Live Above The Hype
Life Skills Student Workbook
4th Edition

Name:

_____

This curriculum is not to be used without the written permission of Inner Sun, Inc.

Live Above the Hype Life Skills Student Workbook

Copyright ©2014, 2015, 2016, 2020 Inner Sun Inc. All rights reserved, including the right to reproduce this book or portions thereof in any form whatsoever.
For information contact Inner Sun, Inc., PO Box 1716, Covina, CA 91722

Fourth Edition
Cover Artwork: Virtually Possible
Book Layout Design By: K-Rahn Vallatine
Book Illustrations By: Ronald "Riskie" Brent & K-Rahn Vallatine
First Edition: May 2014

ISBN-13: 978-0-9916382-7-7

Printed in the United States

www.liveabovethehype.com

Foreword

Stay in Touch

A Word From Dr. Michael Eric Dyson

More than a decade ago, I met a bright, handsome and charismatic young man at Pasadena City College where I had gone to lecture. There were many wonderful students at my talk, but K-Rahn stood out, perhaps because we bonded over West Coast hip hop and the magnetic flow he shared with me in person, and later, on his rap recordings. I was impressed with his artistic talent and sharp mind, but above all, with his patience and persistence in keeping in touch, especially since my busy schedule kept me from reaching out as much as I wanted to, or, to be honest, as much as I should have.

    I knew his generation was being hammered in the media and in cultural quarters across the nation, and particularly in black life, with familiar yet flawed accusations: they're self-destructive, they care little for the community, they're addicted to pathology, they don't give a damn about "our" history, and most dispiriting of all, they're not worth our time. His life and vision were an eloquent rebuttal to the bitter lies and brutal stereotypes that dog black youth the world over.

    K-Rahn never took my unreliable communication as anything but the busy efforts of an elder to get things right for our people and, ironically enough, for his generation. He never took my long sieges of silence personally, never lashed out. He just kept calling, emailing and texting.

    In short, K-Rahn became the mentor he sought out in me; he taught me a great deal about living up to your word, being present for the people you say you love and serve, and uplifting and challenging the people for whom you breathe your gift on earth. His soulful manner and loving spirit spoke louder than even his brilliant rhetoric on record.

    If K-Rahn mentored me, his supposedly wiser elder, and by extension, the generation that came before him, then he's doing even more to mentor the youth who are coming over the path he helped to blaze. This workbook, as he calls it, is rightly named, for it does a great deal of work in helping young people identify their problems, name their obstacles, receive help, and rise above the bewildering social and cultural options that hold out destruction in the name of popularity.

K-Rahn's not only been there and done that, but he's lived to tell a compelling story of overcoming youthful mistakes and has returned with a roadmap to successful survival. And he does it without rancor, finger pointing or a sense of moral superiority, much like he did when he helped to redeem me from a slight case of generational hypocrisy.

In the process of speaking to young folk, he avoids two extremes: he neither beats up on hip hop culture and the values, goals, aspirations and ideals it promotes – though he does brilliantly and patiently unravel the web of half-truth, deceit, and misinformation that is sometimes spun in the name of "keeping it real" –nor does he blithely excuse the harmful influence of some quarters of the culture he clearly loves a great deal. He is supremely balanced in accounting for the glorious beauties that are often ignored in hip hop while keeping his eye on the unfortunate lapses in judgment that mar the rhetorical landscape and lived experiences of our youth. K-Rahn takes note of the cosmic and the practical in this book – he addresses the governing ideals that have shaped a culture that has, in turn, shaped the perception of black youth around the globe, and speaks to the everyday habits and practices that make a huge difference in the lives of young people.

Live Above The Hype is at once a manifesto of independent critical thought, a compendium of wisdom about how to make it through tough times and circumstances, and a love letter to spiritual and personal transformation in the midst of cultural evolution. The book you hold in your hand is the intellectual lovechild of Plato, Oprah and 2Pac. Read it and get a sense of what an extraordinary man K-Rahn is, and why you shouldn't repeat the mistake I made by not keeping in better touch. This book is K-Rahn's personal call to our youth, and to those of us who love them, to think clearer and to do better. This time I'm listening. I hope you will do the same!

Dr. Michael Eric Dyson, named by *Ebony Magazine* as one of the hundred most influential black Americans, is the author of eighteen books. He is currently a University Professor of Sociology at Georgetown University. Dr. Dyson is also a radio host and political analyst for *MSNBC*.

Introduction

As a youth growing up in today's world, I have found that many of you often feel abandoned and betrayed by people and institutions who should be looking out for you. Many of you are in conflict with much of mainstream society. For understandable reasons, some of you hate school, hate the entire legal system and hate the idea of having to work for someone on a traditional 9-5 job. So, you rebel. Some rebel against the educational system (which includes teachers and counselors, as well as the very information being taught in the classroom). Some rebel against law enforcement. And some rebel against our society's workforce.

Many of you have a perspective which revolves around both conscious rebellion and thoughtless, youthful, anti-social behavior. On one hand, you see yourself one day being very rich and successful, but on the other hand you reject mostly all the paths that can realistically lead to such a life (i.e. education, business ownership, investing, etc.). So now what? **You plan to be rich and successful.** Great. What is your plan for achieving this goal? I find many young people approach life similar to a lottery player. Without much work, you hope luck works in your favor and one day your numbers will pop up and you will collect millions of dollars and be set for life! It could happen, but most likely it won't, so I wouldn't bet my life on it! Unfortunately, many people who came before you thought the same way and are now stuck in ruts they do not wish to be in.

This workbook is to be used as a resource to first question yourself as well as to open insightful dialogue that promotes critical thinking. In this workbook, we will analyze the value system that draws many of us to street culture. We will analyze the rewards and consequences of the choices we make based on this value system. We will analyze why we as a community continue to uphold this value system. And we will question what elements of this system should be *kept* and what elements of this system should be *let go*.

This book is to be used as a resource to help transfer wisdom from older generations to the younger, as well as understanding from younger generations to the older. This book is a tool to help bridge generation and cultural gaps.

Table of Contents

Live Above the Hype Session Agreements: 10

***What Is Your Life's Vison (Section I)**..**11**

Goals & Commitment.. 12

The Importance of Being Intentional 13

Goal Setting 14

The Importance of Having a Goal 16

Seed In Soil 17

S.M.A.R.T. GOALS.. 19

Community & Its Values 21

What's your Grind Like? 29

From Nothin' to Somethin'....Self Made 30

Show Me The Money 34

Wolf Hunting & Crack Selling... 37

See it, Believe it, Achieve it. 38

Scared of the Dark... 39

The Power of Affirmations 45

All I Want to Be Is Successful… 47

It's Bigger Than Hip Hop (Section II)..**50**

It's Just Music… 51

The Current State of Popular Music... 52

Censorship in Urban Music... 56

Psychopathic Personality in Music? 60

A Thought on Hip Hop… 62

Caged Eagles 64

Rappers and Prison 65

To You {In Yall's Eyes} 75

Expect Punishment for A Crime 76

Penal Labor 82

What's Really Important To You 85

Gangbanging Religiously 89

Drugs 95

The World Within Us (Section III) *98*

Emotional Intelligence 99

Anger Management 106

Is Anger a Choice? 107

Healthy Relationships 112

Love 113

Let's Talk About Relationships... 115

Each One, Teach One 120

The Stumbling Block & The Fallen Victor 121

The Blueprint (Section IV) *127*

Keep Your Next Move, Your Best Move 128

The 2 Paths 129

If It Don't Make Dollars It Don't Make Sense 131

The 4 Types of Money Makers... 133

Don't Blend In, Stand Out 136

Numbers Don't Lie 137

Music Business Mathematics 141

Legal Hustler 143

Are You an Entrepreneur? 146

Entrepreneurship: My Own Business 149

Know Better, Do Better 151

Entertainers and College 152

Career Research 158

My Chosen Profession 160

Wealth Mindset 161

Generational Wealth 162

Definiteness of Purpose 168

Forward Movement 171

Decisions & Actions 173

The Gate of Obstacles 175

My Goal 178

Glossary…………………………………………………………………………………..180

Dedication

To all the young people who have been falsely taught that there is victory in self destruction.

Live Above the Hype Session Agreements:

1. One person speaks at a time
2. Raise your hand if you have something to say
3. Listen to what other people are saying
4. Speak in first person
5. No mocking or attacking other people's ideas or opinions
6. Respect each other

Section 1

What Is Your Life's Vision?

"How long should I stay dedicated, how long til opportunity meets preparation?"
                    -Nipsey Hussle (Dedication)

Goals & Commitment
(Module One)

Let's Begin

List one *great* thing about you: _____
_____

The Importance of Being Intentional

Metaphor: *a figure of speech in which a word or phrase is not literal, but is regarded as symbolic of something else*

It is important to know that you must purposely steer your life in the direction you want to go. Let's imagine: If you were sitting in the driver seat of a car, riding on the highway and you decided to keep your feet on the gas pedal and let go of the wheel for a long period of time, what would happen?

_____

As the driver it is important that you know where you are driving. Our lives are no different. Using the car example as a *metaphor*, we must constantly keep our hands on the steering wheels of our lives, steer and know where we are going.

- In the above reading what does the car symbolize? _____
What does "We must constantly keep our hands on the steering wheels of our life" mean? _____

Goal Setting

1. In your own words, define the word *goal*: _____
   _____

2. In your own words, define the word *wish*: _____
   _____

3. What's the difference between the two? _____
   _____

"A Man Who Hunts an Elephant Does Not Stop to Throw Stones at Birds."

4. What is the elephant in your life?
   _____
   _____

5. What are the birds in your life?

   - _____
   - _____
   - _____
   - _____
   - _____

The Importance of Having a Goal

Having purpose (or a goal) in life is extremely important. Here's why: Purpose offers *motivation*. The root word of motivation is _____, or a good reason. When you have a purpose, you have a good reason for doing something. Having a good reason for doing something is what creates motivation. When you are motivated about something, you become engaged and want to pay attention to what is being taught and to what you are doing. When you are engaged in and learning about something you are interested in, you feel better about yourself. Feeling better about yourself helps cause you to make healthy decisions over poor decisions. Making healthy decisions leads to positive outcomes in life. Experiencing positive outcomes in life helps boost your confidence to overcome obstacles that come in your life. Overcoming obstacles leads to more positive opportunities coming into your life. More positive opportunities coming into your life leads to more achievement in life. More achievement in life leads to an overall successful life. It all starts with having purpose, or a clear goal!

Think About It: Many of the poor decisions we make in life come from us not finding a strong enough reason not to make the poor decision. Purpose (or a goal) gives us the reason we need to be intentional about avoiding making poor decisions.

Seed In Soil

Simile: a figure of speech often using the words "like" or "as" to compare two unlike things

Have you ever thought about how trees start off as seeds? These seeds, when planted into the ground, has the potential to grow into large trees. No matter how large a tree grows, almost everything that the tree is made of is first contained inside the tiny seed: The roots, the stalk, the branches, the leaves and the fruit. A tiny seed is full of great potential. As humans, we too start off our lives like "seeds" with the potential to grow into greatness!

Other than air, what 3 things does a seed need to grow into a tree?
_____, _____, _____

- _____ represents a purpose/goal to reach towards.

    What purpose are you reaching towards? (Your elephant)
    _____
    _____

- _____ represents an environment that supports your growth

    What environment best supports you in achieving your purpose/goal?
    _____
    _____

- _____ represents knowledge to help you grow and expand

    What type of knowledge or information do you need to help you achieve your purpose/goal? _____
    _____

Sometimes I wonder if the seed knows how much potential is within it before it grows into that mighty tree it's destined to one day be. Remember, you are full of great potential that you may not have even imagined!

S.M.A.R.T. GOALS

Specific - Be very clear. Instead of saying "I want to do better in school," say "I am earning a B or higher in all of my classes on my report card."

Measurable – Make sure your goal can be measured. In the example above, you can look at your report card and determine if your goal was achieved.

Attainable – Keep your goals achievable. For example, if someone is currently doing extremely poorly in school, instead of saying "I will make all A's by next week," think about saying "I am raising all my grades by one letter by my next report card."

Realistic – A goal is often only as realistic as the commitment given to it. Sticking with our previous examples, earning all Bs or higher is only possible if the student is committed to doing what it takes.

Time-limited – Must have a realistic time frame on your goal. It's important to know by when you expect to have your goal accomplished.

What's your S.M.A.R.T. goal? _____

_____

- Is it specific?   ____Y ____N
- Is it measurable?   ____Y ____N
- Is it attainable?   ____Y ____N
- Is it realistic?   ____Y ____N
- Is it time-limited?   ____Y ____N

What specific actions need to be taken to accomplish this goal?

1. _____

2. _____

3. _____

4. _____

5. _____

> **Now write one S.M.A.R.T. long-term goal, mid-term goal and short-term goal.**
>
> - *Long Term Goal* (something you want accomplished about 5 years from now: _____
> _____
>
> - *Mid Term Goal* (something you want accomplished about 3 years from now: _____
> _____
>
> - *Short Term Goal* (something you want accomplished about 6 months – 1 year from now: _____
> _____

𝕿hink 𝕬bout 𝕴t: The thoughts you think, the words you say, the actions you make and the way you carry yourself should all line up with the purpose/goals you have set for yourself in life.

Community & Its Values

(Module Two)

Vocabulary List #1

Aspects	Community		Genocide
Ideology	Observer	Dictate	Values
Revolve	Suburban	Urban	Recreation

Community and Its Values

A **community** is known by both outside **observers**, as well as inside members, by its culture. We know that language and styles are very important **aspects** of culture. However, the most important part of any culture is its **values**. **A value system is a set of moral codes that one uses to measure right from wrong and success from failure.** For example, in some cultures, loyalty is a value that is highly honored. To fall short of being loyal can be looked at as failing. It is a person's value system that decides whether he is in a culture or out of it. Most cultural aspects, such as trends and styles, usually come from this. Though *individuals* make up the community, it is often the community that **dictates** to an individual what his/her value system is to be. Once the value system is in place, it is then used by community members to measure one's worth.

The Definition of Real

1. How does <u>your community</u> describe a person who is considered *"real?"*

   _____   _____

   _____   _____

   _____   _____

2. Do these characteristics lead to a life of failure & hardship or a life of success & peace of mind? Explain.
   _____
   _____

3. How do <u>you</u> describe a person who is considered "*real?*"
   _____   _____
   _____   _____
   _____   _____

4. Do these characteristics lead to a life of failure & hardship or a life of success & peace of mind? Explain.
   _____
   _____

In the many **urban** communities, much of the value system of the youth is based on short lived materialism and competitiveness. Unfortunately, this value system *also* often **revolves** heavily around self-destructive behavior. When the "outdo everyone else" **ideology** of manhood is held as truth, the male marijuana smoker cannot simply smoke weed, but instead must prove that he can smoke more weed than anyone else around him. The same drive is within he who drinks alcohol. He not only drinks alcohol, straight with no chaser, but must also be able to prove that he can drink more alcohol than anyone else. Youthful competitions such as these are not only in urban communities and are actually widespread throughout rural and **suburban** high schools to Ivy League colleges. It is unfortunate, however, that in many urban communities, self-destructive competition does not stop at such **recreational** activities. Under this pattern of thought, the rebellious student outwardly expresses to his peers, a sense of pride in being the *lowest* academic achiever. He laughs at his failing grade and brags about not attending class. The young criminal takes pride in past incarcerations. The player takes pride in not only how many ladies he has gotten in bed, but also in how many ladies he can control, hurt and ruin. The gangsta takes pride in how many people he has shot and/or killed. The thief finds glory in how many people he's robbed in his neighborhood. The dope dealer is proud that he has managed to *flood* (saturate) his own neighborhood with a substance that he knows is deadly. Somehow we've been taught to celebrate our own destruction.

1. What are the top 3 things your <u>community</u> values most?
   #1 _____
   #2 _____
   #3 _____

2. What 3 things do <u>you</u> *honestly* value most in life? (Not people)
   #1 _____
   #2 _____
   #3 _____

3. What do you do to express that you value each of these 3 things?
   #1 _____
   _____

   #2 _____
   _____

   #3 _____
   _____

4. Who or what taught you to place such high value on these 3 things? Explain. _____
   _____
   _____
   _____

5. Do others around you value these things too? Explain how you know.
   _____
   _____
   _____

6. Is placing such a high value on these things leading you to a successful and positive life or an unsuccessful life of pain and hardship? Explain.

_____
_____
_____

7. Describe how your life would look if you did not place such a high value on these 3 things. _____

_____
_____
_____

8. List the 3 <u>people</u> you value most in life? (Specific person)

   Person #1: _____
   Person #2: _____
   Person #3: _____

9. What do you do specifically to express your value for each of these 3 people?

   Person #1: _____
   _____
   _____

   Person #2: _____
   _____
   _____

   Person #3: _____
   _____

10. How does your value on your 3 chosen <u>things</u> affect the lives of the 3 <u>people</u> you value most?

<u>Person #1:</u>_____
_____
_____

<u>Person #2:</u>_____
_____
_____

<u>Person #3:</u>_____
_____
_____

Whoever controls what you choose to value, also controls your behavior in life

Your values define "*success*" and "*failure*" - What you value determines what "success" and "failure" mean to you. How do you define *success* and *failure*?

Success:_____
_____

Failure:_____
_____

1. What type of life do you want to live? Describe what a successful life looks like for you. _____
_____
_____
_____

2. What must you value now to achieve this life?
_____
_____
_____
_____

Be the person today that your future self thanks you for!

𝕴𝖍𝖎𝖓𝖐 𝕬𝖇𝖔𝖚𝖙 𝕴𝖙: The decisions we make, the words we speak, and even the dreams we pursue all revolve around what we value most. Our value system **dictates** our lives. It even influences how we value ourselves! Be wise in choosing what you value most. If what you choose to value enhances your life and makes you and the world around you better, continue in it; however, if what you value most constantly attracts destruction and failure in your life, it is wise to consider not putting such a high value on that thing or those things.

What's your grind like?
(Module Three)

Live Above The Hype

Vocabulary List #2

Allure	Chauvinism	Fulfill	Illusory
Materialism	Prosperity	Progression	Sole
	Transformation		

From Nothin' to Somethin'....Self Made

From the time a human begins to grow in a mother's womb, we are all created to receive. Once born, as babies, very little changes. We remain **sole** receivers. A baby receives food, attention, clothing, care, etc. Babies *only* receive and are totally out of control when their needs are not met. However there comes a time in the life when we get older and are no longer satisfied with only receiving, but instead grow and desire to work to satisfy our own wants and needs. As life continues, we grow even more and are no longer satisfied with only **fulfilling** our own needs, but we also seek to *share* this fulfillment we receive with others.

This can be seen in an example of a picture vs. a puzzle:

> **If someone gave you a picture of a beach you may appreciate it very little. However, if someone gave you a puzzle of the same picture and you put it together, you will obtain a sense of accomplishment and fulfillment and will probably appreciate it more.**

Through hard work and cleverness, we assemble the puzzles of our own success, and hope to one day become the creators of our own happiness. Creating our own joy is a deep desire and need. This is one of the greatest **allures** of street hustling (drug selling, robbing, stealing, etc.): Getting **prosperity** with the satisfaction of being able to say I wanted something, and I went out there and got it myself! I made it happen! This is the great story of the majority of today's mainstream hip hop music. It is a tale of self-**transformation**...Transforming from the victim and receiver into a victor who genuinely earned a prosperous life using the few tools he/she had. *Self-Made as they say.*

This may explain why so many teens and young adults seek quick money rather than investing in their future financial stability. Unfortunately, what many fail to realize is the odds of winning in the streets are extremely imbalanced and the <u>rewards</u> of fast money often cannot be compared to the potential <u>punishments</u> that can come.

For those who like to gamble: If I asked you to shoot dice (craps) with me, would you agree to bet 1,000 dollars of your money against my 10 dollars of my money?
_____

Hopefully you said no. Why not? _____
_____

The fact that you have much more to lose in that bet than you have to gain is probably the reason you would pass on this bet. Unfortunately, in the streets many make bets worse than this every day. The money made street hustling (selling drugs, robbing, stealing, etc.) usually cannot compare to the amount of prison time you can be sentenced to if caught, tried and convicted! I know sometimes it seems like you're left with no other choice, but remember, a true hustler makes sure the pay-off is bigger than the risk. Think about that for a minute.

It is unfortunate that in American society, one is taught that "real" men and women are tougher, more fearless, more self-sufficient, and outdo everyone around them. Due to this fake idea of manhood, many working class people are struck with frustration, misguidance and the burden of trying to live up to **illusory** standards, while struggling to attain authentic adulthood. However, please note, being a man is about more than having money.

Think About It: It has been said that you are not truly rich until you have plenty of something that money can't buy. What are some riches in life that money cannot buy?

1. What non-material things do you want to have in life?
   _____, _____,
   _____, _____

2. What material possessions do you want to acquire in life?
   _____, _____,
   _____, _____

3. Are any of these material possessions more valuable than your freedom? Yes/No? Explain. _____
   _____
   _____

4. Are these material possessions more valuable than your life? Yes/No? Explain. _____
   _____
   _____

5. Are these material possessions more valuable than a relationship with your loved ones? Yes/No? Explain. _____
_____
_____

6. Are these material possessions more valuable than the lives and safety of your loved ones? Yes/No? Explain. _____
_____
_____

7. If you were lying on your death bed, which would you rather have around you: your loved ones or your material possessions? Explain.
_____
_____

8. Which is more important to you, the non-material things you listed or the material possessions you listed? Explain. _____
_____
_____

"Sound crazy? Well it isn't. The ends justifies the means, that's the system. I learned that in school then I dropped out, Hit the streets, checked a grip, and now I got clout."

{Ice-T - New Jack Hustla}

Show Me The Money

The average conversation between parents and children about school usually goes something like this:

Parents: "Go to school."

Child: "Why do I have to go to school?"

Parents: "To get an education."

Child: "Why do I need an education?"

Parents: "To get a good job."

Child: "Why do I need a good job?"

Parents: "You need a good job so you can make money."

NOW...In many urban areas, this is where the conversation usually takes a turn.

<u>Child's Thought</u>: "Oh...I see. I am suppose to go to school everyday for 12-17 years of my life so I can get a education, and then use this education to prove to an employer that I am good enough to work for them at their company and get paid whatever wage they decide to pay me.

I got a better idea! Since this whole thing is about making money, why don't I cut out the middle men (teachers and employers), save myself 15 years of wasted time

and start an illegal hustle and start making money <u>today</u>! I'll probably make even more money than my teachers."

Honestly, this thought makes a lot of sense. The problem is, the consequences attached to these actions are not thoroughly thought through. As a result, many fall into the repeated cycle of criminal life, which includes incarceration, violence, social exclusion, etc. Unfortunately, many people seem to value fast money above investing in a secure financial future.

Through trial and error I have learned that **if the reward does not outweigh the punishment, it is usually not wise to participate in the action**.

<u>Now Let's Think...Process...Then Act</u>

Question:

What dollar amount is worth doing 5-10 years in prison? $_____
What dollar amount is worth doing 10-15 years in prison? $_____
What dollar amount is worth doing 15-20 years in prison? $_____
What dollar amount is worth doing *life* in prison? $_____

Though some may answer "none" to these questions, many continue to risk serving such prison time on a daily basis for a small dollar amount.

Is freedom more valuable than money?

An alternative explanation to the 3 Little Pigs story

Explain this illustration:

_____
_____
_____
_____
_____
_____

Wolf Hunting & Crack Selling

On the hip hop duo Dead Prez's debut album "*Let Get Free*" they have a track entitled "Wolves" which is the intro to the album. On this track a man makes a chilling comparison between the way indigenous people of the Arctic hunted wolves and young urban males selling crack cocaine in the hood.

The speaker explains that the hunter would put blood on a double edged blade. Then they would melt the ice on the ground and stick the handle of the knife in the ice, so that only the bloody blade is sticking out above the surface. A wolf would smell the blood and this of course triggers his appetite. The wolf then follows the aroma of the blood and sees the bloody blade in the ground. It then walks to the blade and licks the blade trying to eat. When the wolf licks the blade, of course, he cuts his tongue, and he bleeds. As his tongue begins bleeding, he thinks he's having a good appetizer and continues to lick and drink and lick and drink. He of course is drinking his own blood and he kills himself!

The speaker continues, stating, *that's what happened with crack cocaine! "You have these young brothers out there who think they are getting something they're gonna make a living with...they actually think that it's something that's bringing resources to them, but they're killing themselves just like the wolf who was licking the blade, and they're slowly dying without knowing it."*

See it, Believe it, Achieve it.
(Module Four)

Vocabulary List #3

vivid	transform	heroic	conquer	mundane
imagination	productive	potential	enchanted	untamed
	hinder	ridicule	accomplish	

Scared of the Dark

As a child, I remember playing in my bedroom for hours throughout the day. Legos and GI Joes were my favorite toys to play with. Using my **vivid** imagination, I would turn my small room into a mini playground. Dressers would turn into mountains for my actions figures to climb and jump from. My closet would **transform** into a cave for my **heroic** toy soldiers to explore and **conquer**. I would even allow my mind to change hi-top basketball shoes into dangerous erupting volcanoes! This is the power of **imagination**. When put to good use it can change the ordinary, **mundane** world around us into an **enchanted** fantasy land. However, when put to bad use, it can change a beautiful garden into a dangerously scary haunted graveyard. Albert Einstein, once stated, *"Imagination is more important than knowledge. For knowledge is limited to all we now know and understand, while imagination embraces the entire world, and all there ever will be to know and understand."* Just like any powerful creation, imagination can be used **productively** or counter productively, meaning it can be used to help you, or to hurt you.

During my childhood, I remember instances when I was in my own home and scared of the dark. I can remember waking up in the middle of the night, thirsty and wanting something to drink. I would get up out of my bed, walk through the living room, into the kitchen, get a glass of water and make my way back to my bedroom. This may sound like a simple and easy task, but to a five-year old kid with a **vivid** and **untamed** imagination, this short walk sometimes became a great journey only meant for the brave. As I looked around my room, I would see a pile of clothes that my imagination would transform into the bloodthirsty monster from the movie I seen my older cousins watching earlier in the day. My imagination would see my closet as a hiding place for the serial killer that I saw on the news. As I exited my bedroom and entered into my living room, my imagination quickly turned our furniture into wild animals waiting to attack me.

Luckily for me, I've never been one to let fear stop me from pursuing my goal. So even in the face of a bloodthirsty monster, a serial killer and vicious wild animals, I still made it to the kitchen to get my glass of water. However, the question I ask myself is "why did this happen?" How could I spend all day seeing a pile of clothes and a child's closet in my bedroom during the day and still allow my mind to be tricked by my imagination during the night? Why was harmless furniture that I see every day, so easily transformed by my imagination into something viewed as a **potential** threat? Many children at some point of their lives seem to have a similar experience. The question is what caused this fear? Was I really scared of a chair, a closet or living room furniture? No. I realize that I, like many others, was not afraid of the dark, but instead was afraid of what the dark may be potentially hiding. I was afraid of the *unknown*.

Though this is a simple example from my childhood that many can relate to, I have learned that fear of the *dark* is not a fear that is easily grown out of. Sure, as you get older you may no longer fear daily household items turning into alien monsters, but the fear of the unknown stays with many of us. As we get older, fear of unwanted possibilities haunts us and **hinder** us from moving forward towards our dreams. Beautiful visions of us achieving our goals quickly transform into scary scenes of us failing. Powerful mental images of success shape shift into thoughts of "I'm not smart enough...I'm not good enough...What if he/she hurts me?...What if I fail?"

If I had never seen the monster in the movie, my imagination probably wouldn't have a monster to fear. Same with our fear of the unknown. Many of us have seen failure, embarrassment and underachievement in the lives of others. Therefore, we fear the same will happen to us. We choose not to dream too big because we do not want to be disappointed.

Some of us make fun of our peers as a way of joking and playing. However, when we put each other down and laugh at each other's dreams, what we are actually doing is potentially creating more fear of the unknown in the person. Some people are motivated by **ridicule** from others and some are shut down by it. Sometimes, when people are scared to try something new, they hear the voice of the person who has once made fun of them in their head telling them they are not good enough to **accomplish** that goal. They hear them laughing and teasing them.

What many people don't know is people usually make fun of others because they don't feel good about themselves. Teasing and finding things wrong with others is a way to make them feel better about themselves. They call their peers "ugly" because they are secretly insecure about their own looks. They call their peers "stupid" because they question their own intelligence. They laugh at the dreams and goals of their peers because they themselves are scared of their own failure. They put others down, hoping to lift themselves up.

Though there is always the possibility that things may not go the way you would like, the darkness of the unknown should not be feared. The unknown is where growth takes place. This is where dreams are created. This is where our personal greatness is often hiding. If we are making decisions each day towards a good future, there are many treasures waiting for us in the darkness of our unknown. It is important that we use our imagination to focus on a hopeful future, instead of allowing our imagination to drift towards thoughts that cause fear, worry and doubt. Both hope and fear require a person to believe that it is real, so why not stay positive and imagine what is good?

1. Have you ever been scared of the dark? _____

2. The author says fear of the dark is really a fear of what? _____

3. What are some things about the unknown that you fear? _____
   _____
   _____
   _____

4. Has this fear helped you or held you back? Explain. _____
   _____
   _____

5. Have you ever wanted to do something, but chose not to try it because you thought you weren't good enough to do it? Explain. _____
   _____
   _____

6. Have you ever wanted to do something, but chose not to try it because you were concerned about what others would think about you? Explain. Y/N
   _____
   _____

It is extremely important to overcome voices that tell you that you can't succeed and listen to the voices that tell you that you can!

7. What do you think Albert Einstein meant when he stated, *"Imagination is more important than knowledge. For knowledge is limited to all we now know and understand, while imagination embraces the entire world, and all there ever will be to know and understand."*? _____
_____
_____
_____

8. Do you agree with this? Why/Why not? _____
_____
_____

9. Do you ever make fun of people and put your peers down? Why/Why not?
_____
_____

10. Do you ever encourage others to reach their goals and dreams? Why/Why not? _____
_____
_____

11. How does putting each other down and laughing at each other's dreams, potentially create more fear of the unknown in a person? _____
_____
_____

12. Do you believe that there are great things waiting for you in the darkness of your unknown? _____

13. What are some things you believe are waiting for you in your unknown?
_____
_____

14. What decisions are you making today, or should be making today, to create a great future? _____
_____
_____

15. Are you choosing to overcome any fears of the unknown? If so, which ones? If not, why not? _____
_____
_____

The Power of Affirmations

Affirm: to state as a fact

What we think, feel and say about ourselves has a direct influence on our behavior and what we expect of ourselves. Affirmations are thoughts or phrases that we command to be true. When we constantly affirm something, we program our mind to believe it. And it's been said by very successful people, whatever the mind conceives and believes it can achieve!

Affirmations require consistency if they are to make a lasting impact on the way you think and feel. Positive affirmations are positive phrases or statements used to challenge negative or unsupportive thoughts. They can be used to help motivate you, draw positive changes in your life or boost up your self image. If you often have negative thoughts about yourself, positive affirmations can be used to resist these thought patterns and over time replace them with positive thoughts about yourself.

> **Take a moment to complete these sentences with positive thoughts.**

I am great at _____

I like who I am because _____

I feel good about myself when _____

I feel happy when _____

I am important because _____

I know I can achieve my goals because _____

I am naturally talented at _____

I have succeeded before at _____

I am proud of myself because _____

I have overcome _____

I am accomplishing _____

Here are some positive affirmations you may consider for yourself:

1. *I am brilliant*
2. *I can achieve my goals*
3. *I am good enough*
4. *I am great being myself*
5. *I can overcome any challenge I face*
6. *I forgive others*
7. *I forgive myself*
8. *I deserve to be happy*
9. *I rise above negativity*

Which above affirmation do you connect with the most?

_____

Choose or create a positive affirmation to tell yourself daily.

_____

All I Want to Be Is Successful...

1. How do you define the word *"Success?"* _____
   _____

2. Identify someone who you consider successful _____
   _____

3. What about their life makes them successful? _____
   _____
   _____
   _____
   _____
   _____
   _____

4. If you had this same success, what would you do? How would you live?
   _____
   _____
   _____
   _____
   _____
   _____
   _____

5. Do you believe you can achieve similar success? _____

6. If so, what do you have to do to achieve it? If not, why not? _____

7. Are you willing to do what it takes to achieve this success? _____

Picture your life in 5 years. Draw a picture of what it looks like. Drawing skills are not important for this exercise. Imagination and focus are what's important.

It's Bigger Than Hip Hop

"And in the 13th amendment, it don't say that we kings,
They say that we legally slaves if we go to the bing"

- Meek Mill (*Trauma*)

It's Just Music...
(Module Five)

The Current State of Popular Music

1. List 5 rappers who's main message is about hustling, violence, sex and drug:

   _____

   _____

   _____

2. List 5 rappers whose main message is about spirituality, community, family, peace, love & respect for others: _____

   _____

   _____

3. Which music is played so much that it has the opportunity to "grow on you?" The first list or the second list? _____

4. If you decided to get involved in the following activities, list what *type of music/ which artist/ which song you prefer to listen to.* (example: studying for a school exam some may choose to listen to: <u>Classical/Beethoven/Moonlight Sonata</u>)

   a) Street Hustling (illegally)

   _____/_____/_____

   b) Attempting to be romantic

   _____/_____/_____

c) Preparing for an aggressive activity (a tournament, weightlifting, etc.)

_____/_____/_____

d) Doing homework

_____/_____/_____

e) During prayer/meditation/self-reflection

_____/_____/_____

5. Why did you match those songs with the listed activity? Do you understand that the music you listen to can have a direct effect on your emotions?

_____

_____

*Note: It has been said that music not only helps express an emotional message <u>to</u> the listener, but also may **<u>create</u>** emotion <u>in</u> the listener. (example: listening to a song that makes you feel sad after hearing it)*

6. What *emotions* and activity do the majority of the songs you listen to promote?_____

_____

7. How does having this emotion constantly promoted, affect your views on life? _____

_____

8. Can a song's popularity grow if it receives more support from the music industry (i.e. music production, promotion, radio play, etc.)?

_____

9. What messages receive the most radio & mainstream video play?

_____

_____

Challenge: If you notice one or two messages and emotions dominating your music of choice, try bringing balance to your playlist. Example: If you only listen to gangsta and party music, try mixing in some socially conscious music, love songs, oldies, gospel, blues, or alternative music. It may be hard at first, because you are not used to listening to other genres, but over time, it may help give you a more balanced thought pattern.

Live Above The Hype

Many say that the reason mainstream Hip Hop lacks social consciousness is because this type of music doesn't sell.

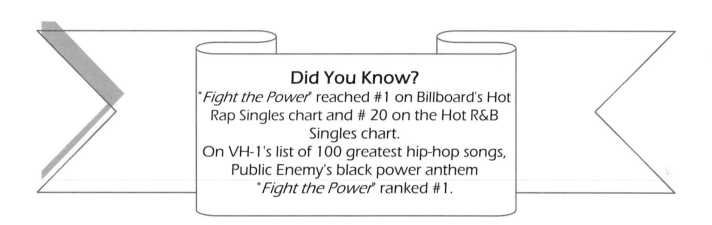

Did You Know?
"*Fight the Power*" reached #1 on Billboard's Hot Rap Singles chart and # 20 on the Hot R&B Singles chart.
On VH-1's list of 100 greatest hip-hop songs, Public Enemy's black power anthem "*Fight the Power*" ranked #1.

"What we got to say,
Power to the people no delay!
To make everybody see
In order to fight the powers
that be!"
-Public Enemy "Fight The Power (1989)"

Think About It: If VH-1, which currently is owned by Viacom, the company who also owns BET, says this is the #1 greatest hip hop song ever, why did songs with lyrical content such as this stop receiving the amount of airtime it once received? Why do songs with opposing lyrical content still receive so much airtime?

Vocabulary List #4

Censor	Controversy	Distribution	Negotiate
Compromise	Criticize	Denounce	Condemn
	Refrain		

Censorship in Urban Music

Censor - *to ban or cut out portions (of a film, publication, song), usually on moral grounds.*

A Few Songs in Hip Hop History Censored By The Media

- NWA released the song "F The Police" and was welcomed with both an official letter from the Federal Bureau of Investigation (FBI) expressing their disapproval, and various threats of police action. Some venues, prior to booking that N.W.A., required unconditional guarantees that they would not perform the song.

"Ruthless a Memoir" by Jerry Heller, SimonSpotlight Entertainment, 2006

- Ice -T (the group Body Count) released Cop Killer - Warner Bros Records ceased manufacturing and **distribution** of the album. The record label then sent out instructions to its distribution company to "inform all music retailers that we would like them to immediately return all unsold 'Body Count' CD's and cassettes for full credit."

New York Times 'Cop Killer' To Be Cut From Ice-T Album' By SHEILA RULE
Published: July 29, 1992; http://www.nytimes.com/1992/07/29/arts/cop-killer-to-be-cut-from-ice-t-album.html

- MTV censors the rap group PUBLIC ENEMY by banning the video for the song called "*Give The People What They Need*" due to references in the song and video to Mumia Abu-Jamal (a political prisoner of the Black Panthers found guilty of killing a police officer in 1981 and initially sentenced to death). Chuck D's people tried to **negotiate** and MTV offered a **compromise**: They can leave the name Mumia in, but they would have to take out the phrase 'Free Mumia' which is in the hook. Chuck D refused to comply.

http://www.411mania.com/music/news/4114/New-Public-Enemy-Video-Banned-From-MTV.htm#JlXHb1iXUSDrzCd6.99 ; http://www.daveyd.com/FNVsept132002.html

- Public Enemy was also previously banned by MTV for the video to the song *"By the Time I Get to Arizona" (1991)*. PE's politically-charged song **criticized** Arizona's rejection towards Martin Luther King, Jr. Day being honored as a holiday. The video was banned by the MTV Standards Department for its portrayal of the assassination of a White supremacist governor.

  http://www.xxlmag.com/news/2011/03/a-history-of-rap-videos-banned-from-tv/

- The Geto Boys' video for the controversial single *"Crooked Officer" (1993)* from the group's *Till Death Do Us Part* was banned by MTV and **denounced** by presidential nominee Bob Dole "due to the images of violence against police officers."

  http://www.xxlmag.com/news/2011/03/a-history-of-rap-videos-banned-from-tv/

- Jadakiss received **controversy** and **condemnation** from political commentator Bill O'Reilly, who labeled him a "smear merchant" due to lyrics in the song, "*WHY*" which suggest that President George W. Bush may have been involved in the September 11th attack on America. "Bush" is censored in *clean versions* of the song. The music video shows a man holding up a picket sign reading "BUCK FUSH." Bill O'Reilly took the position that both the President and others should be allowed to sue Jadakiss for slander. The track was eventually banned on some radio stations or played with the censored lyrics.

  http://en.wikipedia.org/wiki/Why_(Jadakiss_song)
  http://www.foxnews.com/story/0,2933,125675,00.html#ixzz2HVRp6DYL

- Lil Kim, in the song "*Jump Off*," says "my presence is felt like a Black Power movement" and the media censors this segment of the song, yet does not censor the part where she says "*I can make a Sprite can disappear in my mouth.*"

- Michael Jackson's "*They Don't Really Care About Us*" censored because some felt it was anti-Semetic (against the Jewish population).

- Rapper Rick Ross' verse on Rocko's "U.O.E.N.O." was banned from radio stations across the country because of his lyrics which suggested that he "put a molly [pill] all in her champagne and she ain't even know it...[he] took her home and enjoyed that and she ain't even know it." He also temporarily lost his Reebok endorsement due to these lyrics.

1. Why do you think the media censors some songs and not others?
   _____
   _____
   _____

2. Have any artists ever been forced to change the lyrics of a song because they were anti-Black/Brown (against the Black/Brown population)? If so, which ones?
   _____
   _____

3. What are the most common themes promoted in popular rap music these days? List 3 things. _____
   _____
   _____
   _____

4. What are some of the most **uncommon** messages in today's most popular rap music? (Things rappers don't talk about)
   _____
   _____
   _____

5. Why do you think this is?
   _____
   _____
   _____

6. Do you censor the music you listen to? ...Meaning, are there certain songs you refuse to listen to because of the message of the song? Why/Why not?

_____
_____
_____

Think About It: People will often treat you according to what you demand of them. Degrading messages will continue to go forth as long as those being degraded continue to support it.

Challenge: Exercise your will power and **refrain** from listening to, reciting or writing songs with messages of drug use, violence, meaningless sexual encounters, and criminal activity for 1-week.

Psychopathic Personality in Music?

According to dictionary.com, the definition for psychopath is listed as follows:

> *noun*
> *a person with a psychopathic personality, which manifests as amoral and antisocial behavior, lack of ability to love or establish meaningful personal relationships, extreme egocentricity, failure to learn from experience, etc.*
>
> *noun*
> *a person afflicted with a personality disorder characterized by a tendency to commit antisocial and sometimes violent acts and a failure to feel guilt for such acts*

Other researchers associate psychopathy with the following:

> *shallow emotions* (including reduced fear, a lack of empathy, and stress tolerance), *coldheartedness, egocentricity, superficial charm, manipulativeness, irresponsibility, impulsivity, criminality, antisocial behavior, a lack of remorse*, and a *parasitic lifestyle*.

The goal of this section is not to point fingers, but instead to encourage us to be aware and honest about the messages we as a culture seem to heavily embrace and reinforce. With that said, think about this for a moment: **how many songs can you name where the artist expresses traits of a psychopathic personality?**

Name a song that emphasizes each of the following traits:

- **antisocial behavior** (*a behavior that lacks consideration for others and may cause damage to the society, whether intentionally or through negligence*)
  _____

- ***lack of ability to love or establish meaningful personal relationships*** *(unable to allow oneself to be vulnerable enough to deeply care for and trust someone else)*

  _____

- ***extreme egocentricity*** *(self-centered; concerned almost solely with one's own needs, comfort and self-image)*

  _____

- ***failure to learn from experience*** *(continuing to make the same mistakes over again; never learning from them)*

  _____

- ***tendency to commit violent acts with failure to feel guilt for such acts*** *(feeling no pity or shame after inflicting violence on someone)*

  _____

- ***lack of empathy*** *(lacking the ability to feel the feelings of others)*

  _____

- ***coldheartedness*** *(ruthlessness; no care or consideration for the well-being of another)*

  _____

- ***irresponsibility*** *(making decisions with no regard for the consequences; not accountable for one's own actions)*

  _____

- ***impulsivity*** (*acting without thinking it through*)
  _____

- ***criminality*** (*the quality or state of being a criminal*)
  _____

- ***parasitic lifestyle*** (*a lifestyle that feeds almost solely off of the effort of others*)
  _____

A Thought on Hip Hop...

I understand that the beauty of music and entertainment is the ability to take us out of reality for a moment to experience such thrills as those we listed above. Some watch horror movies not because they embrace and celebrate horrific acts, but because it's an escape from reality. Unfortunately for hip hop we know that it is more than music. It is a culture. The music is often used to spread values of the culture. I also realize such values are also reinforced in many other genres of music and forms of entertainment (such as movies and video gaming), and are a very important part of American culture. But in this book, we are focusing mostly on Hip Hop culture.

1. Does the majority of the music you listen to encourage psychopathic thinking and/or behavior? _____

2. What happens when a whole community continually engages in psychopathic behavior? _____
_____

3. Do you think you can have a healthy and peaceful life while embracing a psychopathic personality? _____

4. What do you think living a psychopathic lifestyle usually produces in a person's life? _____

5. Do you think psychopathic personalities eventually fade away naturally, or do you think a person must *consciously* work at changing? _____

Think About It: If the value system that we uphold as truth and continue to promote is psychopathic, where will that lead us?

Caged Eagles
(Module Six)

Rappers and Prison

"Back in November [2009], XXL profiled Lil Boosie, just as he was releasing his forth album, *SuperBad: The Return of Boosie Bad* ---. At the time, the Baton Rouge stalwart was also wrapping his head around a looming two-year bid in prison for marijuana possession. Instead of dreading his pending sentence, Boosie was almost buoyant about the prospect of serving time, even offering that he thought it would help his art and his career. 'I'm taking it like it's a boost to my career. Yeah jail make everybody --- hot.'"

XXL Magazine, March 2010, pg 58, article by Jack Erwin

Question:

Does a rapper going to jail help or hurt his career? Explain.

_____

_____

_____

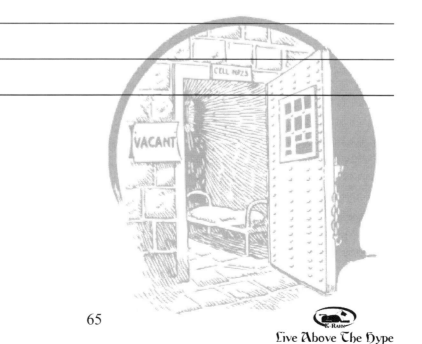

Here is a list of over 40 rappers throughout Hip Hop history who have gone to prison *after getting a record deal.*

Shyne - Served 9 years in prison for assault, criminal possession of a firearm and reckless-endangerment; after prison release, Shyne was deported back to Belize.

Max B (Dip Set) - Sentenced to 75 years on felony murder charges, aggravated manslaughter, kidnapping, armed robbery and conspiracy for orchestrating a robbery that left a man dead.

Gucci Mane - Sentenced to a maximum of one year in prison for a second probation violation stemming from a 2005 assault charge. In 2014 he was arrested for gun related charges.

C-Murder - Sentenced to life in prison for a murder that took place in January 2002. Two weeks later, he received an additional 10 years for two charges of second-degree attempted murder stemming from an August 2001 incident.

2Pac - Sentenced to 1 1/2 - 4 1/2 years on sexual abuse charges (touching a woman's buttocks); He served 11 months.

Project Pat - Served 3 years for weapon charges

T.I. - In 2007 Tip was arrested on gun related charges. He received a year and a day in prison, house arrest and fines.

Lil Kim - Served 10 months in prison for lying under oath (perjury)

Turk (Cash Money) - Convicted of second-degree attempted murder of a police officer. He was sentenced to 10 -12 years.

Da Brat - Sentenced to 3 years in prison, seven years of probation and 200 hours of community service for striking a woman in the face with a bottle.

Prodigy (Mobb Deep) - sentenced to 3 1/2 years behind bars after pleading guilty to a weapons charge dating back to 2006.

Cassidy - found guilty of involuntary manslaughter in the shooting death of a 22-year-old man and sentenced to 11 and a half to 23 months in prison, plus probation. Cassidy was also convicted of two counts of aggravated assault and possession of an instrument of crime for his involvement in the shooting.

Flesh-N-Bone (Bone Thugs N Harmony) Sentenced to 12 years in prison for assault with an AK-47 rifle and being an ex-convict with a gun back in 2000.

Foxy Brown Sentenced to 1 year in jail for violating probation.

J-Dee (Da Lench Mob) - Convicted of murder and *sentenced* to life in prison

Ol Dirty Bastard - Sentenced 2 to 4 years in prison, after having pleaded guilty to cocaine possession

Remy Ma - Sentenced to 8 years in prison for charges of assault, weapons possession and attempted coercion.

Pimp C - In 2002, Pimp C was sentenced to eight years in prison for violating his probation he had received from an earlier aggravated gun assault charge. On December 30, 2005, Pimp C was released from prison and placed on parole until December 2009.

Mystikal - On June 26, 2003, pleaded guilty to sexual battery and extortion. On January 15, 2004, he was sentenced to six years in prison after pleading guilty to forcing his hairstylist to perform sex acts. He also admitted to extortion.

Lil Boosie - He was sentenced to eight years after pleading guilty to drug charges.

Others Include: Lil Wayne, Meek Mill, Tray Dee (Eastsidaz), Ja Rule, 03 Greedo, Young Buck, Rakim, Beanie Sigel, Big Lurch, X-Raided, Chi-Ali, Ras Kas, Slick Rick, Style P (The Lox), Bobby Smurdah, Kevin Gates,

BG (Cash Money), John Forte (Fugees), Kodak Black., Mysonne, Juelz Santana, Loon, G-Dep, AR-Ab. Can you name any others?

_____

_____

1. Of those listed, whose career did going to prison help?

_____

_____

2. Many of those listed at one time had great careers. However, many of them you may not have ever heard of. Do you think them going to prison may have damaged their career? Explain. _____

_____

_____

_____

> "In the long run, jail has destroyed far more careers than it's helped. Tupac and T.I. were able to do brief bids and come out with their momentum untapped, but a host of other artists have seen their careers significantly hamstrung by time behind bars."

XXL Magazine, March 2010, pg 62, article by Jack Erwin

1. Why do you think so many rappers have been to prison after getting a record deal? _____
_____
_____

2. Do you feel rappers must live the life they rap about? Why/Why not? _____
_____
_____

3. How would you feel about a rapper whose life is totally opposite of his lyrical content? _____
_____

4. If a rapper raps about being a gangster, is it smart for him/her to continue living a gangster lifestyle once he/she has a professional rap career? Why/Why not? _____
_____
_____

5. If a professional rapper no longer is living a gangster lifestyle, should he/she stop rapping about gangster themes and rap about his/her true current lifestyle? Why/Why not? _____
_____
_____

6. If you were a professional rapper making a nice living off of your rap career, would you live a gangster lifestyle? Why/Why not?
_____
_____

7. The 1990's rap group Tha Comradz once stated *"You can take the boy out the hood but you can't take the hood out the homeboy."* Do you believe this is true? Explain. _____
_____
_____
_____

8. Can a rapper still be *real* without participating in criminal activity? _____

To You {In Yall's Eyes}

It seems in your eyes I ain't nothin' but a gangbangin' menace
Hangin' and plaguin' our city streets,
But to da' homiez, I'm just a down brotha to the end,
One of the coolest cats you'd ever wanna meet...
To you, I ain't nothin' but dat fast talkin' low-life,
Exploitin' our women and manipulatin' the street corners,
But to my wife, I'm just doin' what's needed to survive,
She knows I'll never put nobody before her...
To yall, I'm dat rappin' millionaire,
Who gots everythang dat money can buy,
But within myself, I'm empty,
Tired of advertisin' and livin' one big lie...
To you, I'm dat mean stranger,
Forever walkin' the streets, holdin' a frown,
But to me, I'm simply a loner in the midst of this cold world,
One who stays in need of a smile...
To yall, I ain't nothin' but a cold hearted prison inmate,
Deservin' to be locked in a cage,
But to my momma, I'm her oldest and closest son,
Simply a child, who drifted from the way I was raised...
To you, I'm dat revolutionary brother,
With all the answers for mental and spiritual correction,
But to my Lord, I'm a humbled child,
A lost soul, in need of His direction...
See, in yall's eyes, I'm just a former slave turned opportunist,
Tryna stand with no man next to me,
But to my people, I'm a descendant of a great nation,
tryin' to continue our great and victorious legacy...

What do you feel is the message of this poem?

_____

_____

Vocabulary List #5

> Discrimination Subjected Exclude Relegate
> Rites Of Passage Lease Emancipation Privatize
> Rehabilitate Restitution

Expect Punishment for A Crime

In hip hop culture and street culture, we highly honor strength, survival and dominance. This may be a reason why, unlike in many other cultures, in hip hop, doing prison time is honored by fans. Those who do time are sometimes respected as a bit more "realer" than those who haven't experienced prison. Throughout the years, prison has seemed to become somewhat of a *rites of passage* in the hood.

Do you feel going to prison is a natural part of life and should be expected? Explain. _____

_____

_____

_____

Have you ever heard of the Jim Crow Laws?

> *Jim Crow laws were state and local laws in the United States, enforced most blatantly in Southern states, that legalized segregation in the quality of life between blacks and whites. It allowed the Caucasian population advantages that were not extended to the African American population. These laws affected education, housing, employment, healthcare, judicial practices, voting rights, recreation, etc. It was said to be ended in 1965 with the signing of the Civil Rights Act.*

Michelle Alexander, author of *The New Jim Crow: Mass Incarceration in the Age of Colorblindness*, explains that:

*IF LABELED AS A FELON, YOU CAN BE **SUBJECTED** TO ALL FORMS OF **DISCRIMINATION** THAT ONCE APPLIED TO AFRICAN AMERICANS DURING THE JIM CROW ERA.*

Think about it for a minute:
ONCE LABELED AS FELON IN THE UNITED STATES,

- ✓ YOU MAY BE DENIED THE RIGHT TO VOTE
- ✓ YOU CANNOT SIT ON JURIES
- ✓ YOU LOSE YOUR RIGHTS TO BEAR ARMS
- ✓ AND YOU'RE OFTEN LEGALLY DISCRIMINATED AGAINST IN EMPLOYMENT, HOUSING, ACCESS TO EDUCATION, AND PUBLIC BENEFITS

*AS A FELON, MANY ARE **RELEGATED** TO SOMEWHAT OF A SECOND-CLASS STATUS MUCH LIKE PREVIOUS GENERATIONS OF THE JIM CROW ERA*

1. According to the reading, what are some ways felons are treated as second class citizens? _____
_____
_____
_____

2. Unless one is able to get his/her criminal record expunged (erased or removed completely) how long does this treatment last for a felon (1-year, 2- years, 5- years, 15- years, life)?_____

3. Do you think it's fair that a person convicted of a crime is punished by the courtroom, and then punished again by society once he/she has served his/her time? Explain. _____
_____
_____

13th Amendment to the U.S. Constitution

Section 1. Neither slavery nor involuntary servitude, **_except_** _as a punishment for crime_ whereof the party shall have been duly convicted, shall exist within the United States, or any place subject to their jurisdiction.

Section 2. Congress shall have power to enforce this article by appropriate legislation.

1. In your own words, what is Section 1 of the 13th Amendment really saying?

   _____

   _____

   _____

2. According to the 13th Amendment, is slavery still legal in the United States? _____

Private Owned Prisons

A private prison or *for-profit* prison, jail, or detention center is a place in which individuals are physically confined by a privately owned company that is contracted by a government agency. Government systems, such as courts, make business deals with these private prison companies to house prisoners and then pay an agreed rate for each prisoner confined in the facility.

In other words, you have heard of State Prisons, Federal Prisons, etc.? There are also Private Owned Prisons which house inmates for a profit.

There are companies who own and operate **privatized** correctional and detention facilities in the United States. Some of these companies are even traded on the New York Stock Exchange. This means people are investing money in the prison industry and seeking to make a profit. Many common products used in our society are made by inmates in prison and sold for a profit. Also, remember, these prison owners also receive money for each inmate housed in the facilities. So, the more prisoners in their facilities, the more profit is made.

What's your thoughts on this?

_____

_____

Convict Leasing

Convict leasing was a system practiced in the Southern United States that provided prisoner labor to paying companies. It had its beginning with the **emancipation** of enslaved Blacks at the end of the American Civil War in 1865.

A private company would **lease** (rent) prison inmates to work for them, usually on a plantation, coal mine or something of this nature. The lessee was responsible for feeding, clothing and housing the prisoners and would often have the prisoner work under extreme work conditions. It is said that convicts who were leased were treated worse than those enslaved. The reason for this was because a slave was bought and had to be kept alive in order for the slave owner to make money off of his investment. Under convict leasing, a prisoner could be worked to death with no loss to the lessee. He would simply lease/rent another prisoner.

1. What is a private owned prison? _____
_____
_____

2. When inmates of a private owned prison make products and they are sold for a profit, who keeps the profit? _____
_____

3. Explain what convict leasing is. _____
_____
_____

4. In what ways are private owned prison labor and the system of convict leasing similar?_____
_____
_____

A calculator may be helpful for this next section...

"I heard him say gang violence is a problem, And he think that more prisons is a step to resolve it, But more prisons means the checks keep revolving, And it don't take a rocket scientist to see the conflict!"

-Nipsey Hussle (Payback)

Penal Labor

Do the Math

1. As a prisoner working at $0.30 an hour, how much money would you make working a full 8-hour day (before taxes)?

   _____

2. At this rate how much would you make working 7-day week (before taxes)?

   _____

3. At this rate how much would you make working a 4-week month (before taxes)? _____

4. At this rate how much would you make working a 12-month year (before taxes)? _____

5. After the court-ordered deductions (restitution/fines) of approximately 50% take place, how much money are allowed to actually keep? _____

So let's look at this. You work a total of approximately 2,920 hours (8 hours per day x 365 days a year) and only pocket $438.00! *(numbers will slightly differ from your answer to #5 because we used a different measure for breaking down the total number of work hours in a calendar year)*

6. As of July 2016, the federal government mandates a nationwide minimum wage of **$7.25** per hour, though many states are higher. How much money would you make working the same number of hours (2,920) at $7.25 (before taxes)? _____

A huge difference right? This number would actually be more because at most jobs, when you work more than 40 hours in one week, it is counted as overtime *pay*. In our prison scenario, you worked **56 hours per week**!

Think About It: Some say they refuse to work a job that pays minimum wage, but often take risks that lead to consequences that cause them to end up working for much less.

What's Really Important to You?
(Module Seven)

Phases of Life - List what a person mostly does in each of the following phases

BABY	CHILD	YOUNG ADULT	ADULT

1. Of what you listed, what is usually a baby's top priority?
   _____

2. Of what you listed, what is usually a child's top priority?
   _____

3. Of what you listed, what is usually a young adult's top priority?
   _____

4. Of what you listed, what is usually an adult's top priority?
   _____

5. Age does not always determine which phase of life you are in. Since babies, children, young adults and adults do much of the same things, what determines what phase you are in - in life?
   _____
   _____
   _____

6. At this point in your life, which phase of life are you in?
   _____

7. In your own words, what does it mean to be an adult?
   _____
   _____
   _____

Remember, getting older is a natural part of life, but growing up is a choice.

Datz Wassup

LORD help us, the city went loco, it seems gangbangin got tha hood in a chokehold.

Nobody wanna make the slow doe they rather bust tha 4-4 shake tha po-po and stay low pro.

See pops was a no show, school was a no-go, now I'm on tha turf with these grown folks.

My elders told me, slow down homie, but the hood is what I know and they stay down for me.

You say I need to be respectful and check the way I act, but my mother's brother's beggin me for crack.

My older brother's handin me a strap homie what should I do, see the first crack baby just turned 42.

I'm not treated like American, I go to school you pumpin me wit retalin, I'm feelin like a veteran on heroin.

I wanna make a change and free my soul but LORD you put me here and all I know is stick to the code.

{Lyrics by K-Rahn}

Vocabulary List #6

| Anthem | Deity | Devotion | Martyr | Moral |
| | | Ritual | Libation | |

Gangbanging *Religiously*

"[They] outta line how they came through, Shot em in his face point blank left his brains blew, Now who gone go for em, Probably be the same crew, When bangin is yo religion it's like it's sin not to"

{Nipsey Hussle - The Hustle Way}

Religion is said to be the belief in and worship of a god or gods, or any such system of belief and worship, usually involving **devotional** and ritual observances, and often containing a **moral** code governing the conduct of human affairs. Some parts of religion are narrative (stories), symbolism, beliefs, and practices that are supposed to give meaning to a person's experiences of life.

With that definition stated, it seems gangbangin' has become a religion for some. It seems that for those who are heavily committed, the hood or gang has become somewhat of a **deity** to its members. Some believe, or claim they believe, that they are truly living for a noble cause and living & risking one's life for the hood is their purpose in life. "Born to bang." *The hood* is raised above all else. Devotionals (hood **anthems**) are played and recited. **Rituals** are conducted: hood dances are shared, special handshakes, hand motions and languages are used, special "holidays" are observed, **libation** is poured to honor the dead/**martyrs**, etc. Codes of expected conduct are expressed and taught by the hood's elders...the big homies. Stories about the hood are passed down from generation to generation. Gang symbols are written, tattooed and spray painted. Human sacrifice of innocent bystanders and rival gang members are offered in the name of the hood. Yes, for some, it seems like gangbangin' is a religion. As people, most of us thirst for something bigger than ourselves to believe in and live for. We need family, community and acceptance. And it seems for some, "the hood," and the *lifestyle* that it offers, are quick to fill this void.

Gang culture is now a very influential part of pop culture. So whether you are personally involved in this life or not, it's a good idea for us to have a discussion about it.

Gangbangin'

Do what you gotta do but know you gotta change, gotta find a way to make it out tha game! {Makaveli/2Pac, Blasphemy}

1. Generally, what was the original purpose for the organization of many of the groups we now refer to as "street gangs?"
    a. to kill enemies
    b. to join forces to protect one's neighborhood from racist terrorism
    c. no reason...*just to bang tha hood*

2. What is meant when a gang member says "*my hood*?"
   _____

3. If the gang member owns no property in "his/her" hood, does it really belong to him/her? Explain.
   _____
   _____

4. What is a landowner?
    a. a person who owns the land
    b. a person who lives on the land
    c. a person who hangs out on the land

5. What must happen when the landowner of the hood raises the rent too high for his/her tenant to afford?

   _____

6. What would happen if all the landowners of the hood raised the rent too high for all current tenants to afford?

   _____

7. Is there a special cause that most gangs are fighting for? How does one's gang win? What is the realistic end goal of gangbanging?

   _____

   _____

   _____

8. What must a *true* gang member be willing to give up for *the hood?* What does he/she receive in return?

   _____

   _____

   _____

9. What are the 2 most common end results of the gang lifestyle?
   a. retirement with a pension and medical benefits
   b. prison and/or a violent death
   c. fame and millions of dollars

10. Who usually suffers most when a gang member is killed or goes to prison?

    a. tha homies

    b. family and *very* close friends

11. If you were to get caught up and had to do a long term prison bid, let's say 15 years or more, how many of your *homies* do you think would write you, visit you, put money on your commissary, and/or help take care of your family throughout your **entire** bid? _____

12. How long do you think your *homies* would write you, visit you, put money on your commissary, and/or help take care of your family? _____

13. Being honest, how long do you think you would write, visit, put money on commissary, and/or help take care of your *homie's* family who's doing a 15 year or more bid? _____

14. If you put in work for the hood, and was caught and sentenced to life, do you think once behind prison walls you would feel the hood was worth it, or do you feel you would have regret? Explain. _____

_____

_____

15. Is *your hood*/community worth you losing your life?

_____

16. What would be the main thing you would want to be remembered for if you died for *the hood*?

    _____

17. Is it wise to play a game where there is no possible way to win?

    _____

18. As a gang member, would you want your son and/or daughter to be from your gang? Why or why not?

    _____

    _____

19. Would you want your son and/or daughter to marry an active gang member? Why or why not? _____

    _____

20. Is it possible to love your hood/community and still respect others from communities outside of yours? _____

Vocabulary List #7

Detrimental	Impulsive	Deceptive	Euphoria
Perspective	Procrastinate	Frequency	

Drugs

I'm sure we've all heard the phrase "Say No to Drugs." Drug use can be very **detrimental** to one's bodily and mental health. And depending on one's drug of choice, can even be deadly. Our discussion regarding drugs is not focused on the medical effects drugs may have on one's brain, lungs, liver, skin, heart, etc. There is much information around for you to do research on such topics. Instead we will briefly be discussing drug use's effects on one's personality, image, decision making and opportunities.

Many people use drugs socially, to have fun. Some smoke their drug of choice; some drink their drug of choice; some swallow their drug of choice; and some sniff their drug of choice. Some even combine these methods. If you use drugs how does your drug of choice affect your personality? Drugs have a way of molding a user's personality. Over time, some drugs may make you more violent than usual...or more short tempered with people around you. Sometimes your drug of choice may make you more distant from people or even weird around people. Though you may enjoy the high, your drug of choice may make you more reckless and careless...or even lazy. If you have built an addiction to your drug of choice, it maybe has even made you more **deceptive**, even toward your own loved ones. Those few minutes or few hours of **euphoria** can potentially lead to very strong effects on your personality!

Drug use can also affect the **perspective others have of you**. We may say we do not care about what others think about us, but in a world where your "network" can help determine your "net worth," certain people's perspective of you counts greatly. You've probably heard "It's not what you know, but who you know." I'll take it a step further and say, "**It's not who you know, it's who knows you!**" and how they view you. Regardless of how cool you may seem to some, anyone who has authority or power in society views a drug addict as irresponsible. Your favorite rapper may rap about heavy drug use and reckless lifestyles; however if he/she invited you to a multi-million dollar business meeting, in what mindset do you think he expects you to arrive in? Loaded or sober? If he finds out you have a habit you cannot kick what **perspective** do you think he will have of you business wise? Do you think he will still fully trust you to make wise decisions?

Remember drug use can affect your **decision making**. Depending on one's drug of choice and **frequency** of use, one may easily become a **procrastinator**. Have you ever had something important to do, and then got high and said "I'll do it later"? Unfortunately one finds out that later often never comes! "I need to look for a job"...*Puff...Puff*..."Ah...I'll do it tomorrow." "I need to call so and so" ...*Sip ...Sip*... "Ah...I'll call him later." "I'm going to school"...*sniff....sniff*...."Nah...school is lame. Let's party."

Drug use can also have the opposite effect and make one very **impulsive** and careless. Again depending on one's drug of choice after getting high one may act on the first thought that comes to one's mind without thinking it through. Many crimes are committed due to drug use. Many inmates wake up in cold cells asking themselves "Why did I do that?" Many relationships are damaged or destroyed because someone under the influence spoke or acted on the first wild and reckless thought that came to mind.

Again, this discussion is not about the long list of effects that drug use may have on your body and physical well-being. This is about its effects on your life and *opportunity*. Do not let drugs get in between you and your success. Evaluate yourself. If you are a drug user, evaluate your habit. Be honest with yourself.

1. How can using drugs affect your personality and the way you deal and behave with others? _____
_____

2. How do you think drug use can affect the way others view you? Explain.
_____
_____

3. Do you feel drug use positively or negatively affects your decision making?
_____
_____

4. If you use drugs, what type of decisions do you make when you are sober versus when you are under the influence? _____
_____
_____

5. Does drug use personally interfere with your opportunities for success? Yes/No? Explain. _____
_____

"Memories of adolescent years there was unity, but after puberty we brought war to our community."
-2Pac *(Never Be Peace)*

Emotional Intelligence
(Module Eight)

Emotional Intelligence

Did you know that a person's level of intelligence can go beyond critical thinking, academic knowledge and book smarts? Have you ever met someone who is great at seeing other's points of view? Or a person who is extremely patient, understanding and forgiving? Or a person who is great at understanding what you mean even if you don't clearly say it? These people probably have high levels of emotional intelligence. Emotional intelligence is the ability to be aware of, control and express one's emotions, as well as the ability to healthily interpret and respond to the emotions of others. This requires empathy, the power to see the world through the eyes of others.

So we're clear, emotions are feelings or a state of mind we have that are usually in response to circumstances, moods, or interactions with others. Some people are naturally gifted in the way they understand and deal with their emotions and the emotions of other people, while others may need help in this department.

To develop such intelligence, we must learn to be in tune with our thoughts and feelings and look at ourselves in an honest way. Challenging our own thoughts and feelings is a good way to start. We can ask ourselves questions like:

- Am I thinking the right way?
- Should I have used those words?
- How would I have reacted if I were in his/her shoes?
- Is there another way of looking at the situation?
- What reactions are my words and actions attracting?
- Is this the best way to respond?

Learning the language of emotions help us to have healthier relationships in life.

1. What is emotional intelligence? _____
   _____
   _____

2. What is empathy? _____
   _____

3. Think of a time when asking yourself the previous questions could have helped prevent a negative situation. Explain the situation and how it could have helped. _____
_____
_____

Remember, what we've been taught along with the experiences we've had in our lives help create the opinions, beliefs and perspectives we have about the world around us. What we've been through and been exposed to, greatly influences who we are, what we say and how we behave.

4. Can you think of a time when you felt like you were right for being angry at a person and then later saw the situation from a different point of view? _____

5. What caused you to see the situation from a different point of view? _____

6. How did seeing things from this point of view affect the way you felt about the situation? _____
_____

7. When a conflict arises, do you think it's good for people to attempt to see things from each other's view before reacting? _____

8. Why/Why Not? _____

9. Has someone ever been angry with you because of your words or actions? _____

10. If so, please describe what happened. _____
_____
_____

11. Do you think if you could get them to see the situation from your point of view they would feel differently? Explain. _____
_____

According to Daniel Goleman, author of the book, *Emotional Intelligence*, emotional intelligence has five parts:

- <u>Self-awareness</u> – the knowledge of what we feel and why we feel so
- <u>Self-regulation</u> – the ability to express our feelings in a healthy way
- <u>Motivation</u> – the inner drive to change the way we feel and express
- <u>Empathy</u> – the ability to see the world from other's perspective
- <u>Social skills</u> – the ability to communicate effectively and build strong connections with others

In learning emotional intelligence, it is important to be aware of which parts of emotional intelligence we should be working on. Some of us may have great social skills but struggle with self-regulation, while others may be high on self-awareness but poor in empathy.

12. Which one from the list do you feel you are strongest in?
    _____

13. Which one from the list do you feel you are the weakest in?
    _____

14. Which one from the list do you feel you should work on building first? _____

In becoming an emotionally intelligent person we must develop the ability to recognize our own emotions and identify how we are truly feeling and why. Some of us are disconnected from our emotions and may not be all the way clear about what we are feeling. Sometimes we may think we are angry, when really, we may be sad and just not allowing ourselves to feel the emotion of sadness. When we get clear about the true emotions we are feeling, we may also get clear about the root cause of the emotions and hopefully address it in a healthy manner.

Managing our own thoughts and feelings and being able to express them in a healthy manner are very important parts of gaining emotional intelligence.

Why is it we sometimes do not recognize our true emotions?

_____

_____

The truth is, we only have control over ourselves and no one else. Keeping this in mind, it's also important to develop the ability to understand others' emotions. Doing this can help us to not be so quick to take the behavior of other's personal. Remember, most people's behavior has very little to do with you and who you are and a lot to do with them and who they are.

Giving others your full attention when they are speaking and listening with a sincere intent to understand, can help with becoming emotionally intelligent. This is called active listening. When listening in this way we also begin to recognize nonverbal messages a person may be expressing. This allows us to gain even more understanding about what the truth of a situation may be. Having this insight can help us to respond to the situation instead of just reacting to people's words and behaviors.

What does the last sentence in this passage mean?

_____

_____

Challenge: **Write a poem that relates to our discussion about emotional intelligence. It can relate any way you choose.**

Tips that may help:

- Think about the message you want to express
- Maybe use metaphors and similes (symbolism and comparisons)
- It doesn't have to rhyme
- Consider the five senses (sight, hearing, touch, smell and taste) and be descriptive when sharing your message

Anger Management
(Module Nine)

Vocabulary List #8

Alternative	Appropriate	Dominate	Effective
Internal	Confrontational	Judgment	External
Productive	Provoke	Meditation	Aggressive

Is Anger a Choice?

Question: Has someone ever made you angry? I know that sounds like a silly question, but stop and think about that for a moment. Has anyone ever really *made* you angry? Does a person have the ability to MAKE you angry? And if so, who gives them this power over your emotions? Answer: You give them this power!

Understand, in many cases *anger is a choice*. Though sometimes our feelings get the best of us, we can control how we respond to our feelings. No one has the power to **dominate** your emotions unless you give them this power. With each action taken we have the power to choose how we will react to it or even feel about it. Some say anger is a learned behavior because many of the things we get angry about come from the way we were taught. What this means is we were taught that we are supposed to get angry about certain things. Example, many of us were taught, if someone does something that we perceive as disrespect, the expected response is get angry. As a matter of fact, if someone disrespects you and you don't choose to get angry, many are taught that this is a sign of extreme weakness. However, what many are not taught is you do not have to be angry to properly deal with and put an end to disrespectful behavior. You can address what offends you without choosing to be angry. This is actually more **effective** since anger usually clouds a person's **judgment**. A trained boxer does not have to be angry to fight; a trained lawyer does not have to be angry to argue his/her point; a trained martial artist does not have to be angry to defend him/herself.

In between the moment someone says/does something that offends you and your reaction to their words/action, there is a split second where you can either choose to deal with the situation angrily or choose another **alternative**. No one can make you angry. They can only do things that you *choose* to get angry about. Though it does take practice, understand you have power over your own emotions.

We must understand that anger is a normal human emotion. However, when it gets out of control it can quickly become destructive and cause major problems in your life. Anger is used by some as a natural response to feeling threatened because it often causes **aggressive** feelings and behaviors which somewhat empowers a person to defend oneself when attacked. Unfortunately, if not properly checked, these same aggressive feelings and behaviors may arise when not being attacked, but when simply being annoyed or when things are not going in the way you expect them to go. When this happens, anger is misplaced and can quickly lead to problems.

People who have learned to properly deal with anger do so in various ways. As stated before, some choose to directly address the matter that offends them in a non-threatening way. They make it clear that they are not pleased with one's words or actions and express what they expect in the future. The key is that they do this without attempting to hurt or offend anyone else in the process. This method can be very healthy, but in doing this, there is still a chance that another person may get upset with you for expressing how you feel. This also is natural. However, when this happens, we must keep in mind that we cannot control the emotions of someone else. If you've sincerely expressed your feelings with no intentions of **provoking**, offending or hurting others, you have done all that you can do in this matter.

Understand that every matter may not be serious enough to be addressed in this way. Being upset with a stranger, who *accidently* stepped on your shoe in a busy arena and quickly apologized probably should not be dealt with in a **confrontational** way. It is not necessary to track him down and express to him how you felt about the situation.

Some choose to "suppress" their anger. This means that they hold their anger inside and attempt to redirect their thoughts and/or actions. So instead of addressing the issue that led to the anger, they simply choose to ignore it and do something else more **productive**. This may be healthy for minor situations such as the shoe example we just mentioned. This may not be very healthy when dealing with serious situations. Constant suppression of anger can cause you to become a bitter person, which means you are always mad about something even when there seems to be nothing to be mad at. It can make you a hostile person, the type of person who is overly aggressive almost all the time. It can also lead to health problems such as high blood pressure, so be careful.

Another way people properly deal with anger is by self-calming. This method is used to both control your outward expression of your anger and also your inner feelings and emotion. Techniques used for doing this consists of **meditation**, counting from 10-1 or 1-10, deep breathing, etc.

Self-talk may also be included in this technique. Self-talk words, phrases or conversations that we silently say to, or have, with ourselves. Our inner conversations can have a great impact on how we feel, think and respond. The key is in being intentional that what we say to ourselves is of a positive and calming manner. For example, instead of saying "if he says one more word, I'm punching him in the mouth," you may say "It's not worth it. I'm not going to let what he says control my actions."

Remember that anger can often be a very natural response to the world around us. However, you have the power over how you express these emotions. There may be certain instances when you may feel anger is appropriate and justified. That is a choice that is in your power. No one can *make* you feel any type way. Furthermore, it is also a crucial choice as to how you choose to respond to this anger.

1. Remember, your body talks to you. What are some warning signs your body sends you to let you know you are starting to get angry? (rapid heartbeat, eye twitching, etc.)
   _____
   _____

2. Can you think of some good reasons to be angry? If so, give an example.
   _____
   _____

3. Has anger ever made your situation better? Explain/Give an example.
   _____

4. Has anger ever made your situation worse? Explain/Give an example.
   _____
   _____

5. Who do you feel is stronger, a person who is easily angered or a person who does not get angry very easily? Explain.
   _____
   _____

6. The author states "we were taught that we are *supposed* to get angry about certain things." Can you think of any examples?
   _____
   _____

7. How do you deal with your anger? Do you address it, suppress it or use self-calming techniques? _____

8. Sometimes people choose to suppress their anger towards big and serious issues and confront small and minor issues. Do you think this is a good way of dealing with anger? Explain. _____
   _____
   _____

9. Which of the 3 techniques used to cope with anger do you feel is the most effective (suppress, confront, self-calming)? Explain. _____
   _____
   _____

10. After reading this short essay on *Anger*, do you think the author views anger as wrong? (hint: reread the last paragraph)
    _____
    _____

11. What is the author's main point regarding anger? _____
    _____
    _____

Anger - The Fly or The Lion

When it comes to dealing with anger, I put situations in two categories: A fly or a lion. Imagine sitting in your living room on a hot summer day watching TV, when all of a sudden, an annoying fly starts flying around you. You try to swat it with your hand but it's too quick. You're so irritated by the fly that you stand up and start following it all around your living room, chasing it with a fly swatter. As it flys around your home, while attempting to hit the pesky insect, you knock over the lamp. Then you knock down your big screen television...then you break the glass table. And then, finally, with a strong swing of fury, you hit the fly with the fly swatter and kill it! You got him! You look around your living room and see the cracked lamp, the broken television and the shattered table. All of this damage just to get rid of a tiny fly. Do you think it was worth it?

_____

Now let's use this same scenario and replace the fly with a lion. If you were sitting in your living room on a hot summer day watching TV and all of a sudden, a roaring lion was in your home, would it be ok to knock over the lamp, television and table trying to conquer the lion and protect yourself from danger? _____

The point is, know the difference between situations that arise in your life that only annoy you and those that are an actual threat to you. Just because something or someone irritates you does not mean it is worth causing long term damage in your life or their life. Many situations that anger us are "flies," but we treat them like "lions."

Live Above The Hype

Healthy Relationships
(Module Ten)

Love

Love is the commitment to the well-being of someone. Before we love others, we must first learn to love ourselves. Sometimes, we as people say that we are committed to our own well-being, but we mean it in a very selfish way. We are committed to our well-being at the expense of others. Some people hurt and damage the lives of others just to make sure that they themselves are ok. These types of people are called opportunists. Opportunists do not consider the well-being of people; they only see the benefit of the opportunity they can receive.

For example, there are some individuals who choose to break into people's houses in order to make money. As they sneak into someone's home and go from room to room grabbing and stealing what they can, they usually don't consider the damage being done to their victim. They do not consider how hard the person may have had to work to buy the things that they are now stealing. The do not consider the fear the children living in the house will experience knowing that a stranger broke into their home. They do not consider how bad it feels to have someone enter into a person's home, the place where a family is supposed to be safe, and have their possessions stolen. All the opportunist chooses to see is that they want money and once they successfully break into a home and come out without being caught, they'll have what they want. The same applies with the way we treat others.

Some enter relationships only seeing what they can gain from the relationship. Therefore, they get involved in friendships, courtships and business partnerships focused only on how they can benefit. They do whatever they need to do and say whatever they need to say in order to get what they want, regardless of how it affects others involved. They are committed to their own well-being, but in a selfish way.

Others who love themselves are committed to their own well-being in a way that is healthy for everyone involved. They make decisions that are best for them, but that does not intentionally harm anyone else. For example, they may choose to go to school to better themselves because they are committed having a successful future. They may choose to avoid drug use because they care about their health and their opportunities in life. They make sure they are well taken care of but not at the expense of others.

Are you committed to your own well-being? _____
If so, in loving way or a selfish way? If not, why not? _____
_____

Some mistake love for obsession. They may have such strong emotions for a person that they think about the person constantly in a possessive way. Because they have such an emotional attachment to the other person, they are not committed to the well-being of the person, but instead, they want to control them. They get angry when the other person does not respond the way they want. They become easily jealous and fear losing the other person. They may even become abusive and blame their emotional outburst on love. Some constantly take from the person they say they love, while giving little in return. However, as a reminder, love is a person's commitment to the well-being of the person they say they love. This includes friendships, family relationships, intimate/romantic relationships and business relationships.

1. According to the definition of love in this book, would you say that you love others? _____

   If so, who? If not, why not? _____
   _____

2. What qualities do you want in a spouse or a partner that you are in a relationship with?

   _____   _____
   _____   _____
   _____   _____

3. What qualities do you think the person you described would want in a spouse or a partner that they are in relationship with?

   _____   _____
   _____   _____
   _____   _____

4. Are you willing to develop these qualities in yourself? _____

Vocabulary List #9

Dysfunction	Doctrine	Reinforce	Mantra	Legacy
Manipulate	Opportunist	Deteriorate	Divisive	Disperse
		Standard		

Let's Talk About Relationships

Since the beginning of human's existence, the relationship between Man and Woman has been the cornerstone of human civilization. It is by way of this union that the human population has been able to reproduce and thrive. However, the idea of what is considered standard has changed throughout the years. In recent times, we see more and more children being raised by single parents, grandparents, same gender unions, and the foster care system. In many communities, the idea of a father and mother headed household is becoming less and less common. Many children, including myself, grew up in neighborhoods where it was very rare to find a home with both a father and mother raising their children together. In high school, none of my friends had a father in their home.

Not having a father in our households left many of us as young men to live life without a blueprint for manhood. With little to no instruction from our fathers regarding true manhood, we were forced to figure it out on our own. We looked to uncles, older brothers, cousins, big homies, and rappers as a model for who we were to become. Unfortunately, many of them grew up in **dysfunctional** homes, as they share in their music, so they often further taught us dysfunctional principles.

Coming up we were taught falling in love was an act of weakness. We held many hip-hop **mantras** as **doctrine**: "G's up, (*bleep*) down; trust no (*bleep*), etc." Our street teachers didn't invent these thoughts, but they did **reinforce** them to my generation. And my generation has done the same by reinforcing these same dysfunctional principles to the next generation. And right before our eyes, our respect for one another continues to **deteriorate**.

The cornerstone of a community is its family structure. If the families are destroyed, the community will be destroyed. If our communities are destroyed, our society will be destroyed. I have found that many young men and women with families, at some point struggle to value and honor the healthy intimate relationships. Few of us were truly taught that as a man, we are not to take pride in disrespecting women. Instead of attempting to break a woman down, it is our position to seek to build her up. Instead of attempting to bring pain and confusion into the lives of others, it is our position to seek to help provide protection and hopefully help offer as much clarity as we can. Instead of being an **opportunist**, who is only in a relationship to see what we can gain materially, it is good to seek to be a provider. And vice versa. Though we may not obtain perfection in this, it is wise to seek such values if we are to have healthy relationships, healthy families and healthy communities.

In the reading it states, *"Instead of being an opportunist, who is only in a relationship to see what we can gain materially, it is good to seek to be a provider."* In your own words, explain what this means.

_____

_____

_____

Many seem to be waiting for the world around them to change before they decide to change. Such a world change will only happen if the individual people change. Including you! We are often taught to love no one and trust no one. But healthy relationships can never be established with such a **divisive** value system in place. I do not encourage that you blindly and foolishly give people your intense love and trust, but let's not consider love and trust as something we *never* give. Instead of not trusting people at all, how about observing the people around you and then deciding how much trust you should give that person and what should you trust that person *with*? Remember, love is not just about emotions, it is a commitment; **a commitment to the well-being of another person**. When dealing with relationships, we should not rule out love, but instead, let's carefully select how committed we are willing to be to the well-being of another. Because many of us fear being hurt or betrayed, we rule out trust and love. However, love and trust are ok. Just be wise in how you share them with others.

Relationships

1. Name 5 songs that promote a healthy family relationship.
   _____
   _____
   _____
   _____
   _____

2. Do you think it's OK to fall in love? Explain. _____
   _____
   _____

3. List 5 characteristics/qualities that you think a good spouse should have. _____
   _____
   _____
   _____

4. List 5 characteristics/qualities that you think a good husband should have. _____
   _____

5. What is the role of a boy/girlfriend, husband/wife and father/mother?

   Boy/girlfriend: _____

   _____

   Husband/wife: _____

   _____

   Father/mother: _____

   _____

6. Describe what you think a healthy marriage looks like.

   _____

   _____

   _____

7. How many healthy marriages have you seen in your life?

   _____

8. Do you want to get married? Why/Why not?

   _____

   _____

9. Do you want your children to be raised with the same family structure as you were raised? Explain. _____
_____
_____
_____

10. What do you think was the main point of the reading?

a. The cornerstone of a community is its family structure. If the families are destroyed, the community in turn will be destroyed.

b. Because many of us fear being hurt or betrayed, we rule out trust and love

c. Instead of breaking a person down who we are in a relationship with, it is our position to seek to build them up.

Challenge: In order for a community to be strong, it must have strong family structures in it. Write a short essay about the type of **legacy** you hope to have? Do you want to have children? What types of lives do you want your children to live? What type of man/woman do you want to be known as by your future household and community? Healthy relationships are important in having a great and balanced home and legacy.

Each One, Teach One
(Module Eleven)

Vocabulary List #10

Marathon	Caliber	Agile	Obstacle	Calamity
Dialogue	Bitterness		Contempt	Intrigued
Honor	Acknowledge	Ironically	Allegory	Parable

The Stumbling Block & The Fallen Victor

Imagine, together as a team, you and other young men and women are running in a **marathon**. In this marathon, you all run side by side. Your goal is to complete the course *as a team*. On your team, there are runners of many different **calibers**…fast, slow, **agile**, clumsy, trained, untrained, and so on. In this marathon, your team is positioned side by side ready to run. In the center of the course, is a huge rock, *a stumbling block*. During the event, the more skilled teammates able to go around or over the block and miss this **obstacle**. Many teammates who are well positioned in the race also avoid the stumbling block. As the marathon continues, some of your teammates who are positioned in front of the block run into it. Of course, they trip and fall. Throughout the race, many who fortunately avoid much of the **calamity** caused by the block begin to laugh at, mock and lose respect for the runners who have fallen. Of those who fall, there is one on your team who, in spite of his busted knee, twisted ankle, and broken pride, rises back up and finishes the marathon. After he finished the marathon, he speaks to upcoming runners about his experience during the run, and his views of the run. Of course, those runners who have also fallen listen. This fallen victor is now the *People's Champion*. Interestingly, when the teammates who avoided the block try to speak to the upcoming runners, one question is asked: *"If we're in this race* *together, why didn't you come back to help remove the block?"* As a result, very few listen to the wisdom shared by the runners who avoided the block. **Dialogue** is cut off. The fallen victor continues to speak, and the runners continue to listen. They relate to the **bitterness** in his voice. They agree with his anger and rebellion. He speaks not only of his pain and suffering during his fall, but also of the glory in his fall and the rejection he got from the runners who didn't fall. After listening to his voice, many of the fallen runners are now less ashamed of their own fall. They don't feel so bad about their current position in the race. In fact, some are so **intrigued** by the story of the fallen victor that they themselves purposely *run toward* the stumbling block and trip over it even when they don't have to. **Honor** is now given to tripping over the stumbling block and many now believe that the block is what made the fallen victor such a great runner. Very few runners listen to those who avoided the block. Dialogue has been so severely cut off that many of the runners who avoided the block now have very little understanding of the fallen, or of those who sadly chose to fall on purpose. **Ironically**, few ask the fallen victor why he never came back to help remove the stumbling block. Instead, the way of the stumbling block is now unfortunately the *hope* of many of the approaching runners.

*This **allegory** is about the urban community, which are the runners; the negative things in this community such as drugs, violence, poor educational systems, poor housing, prison pipelines, etc., which is the stumbling block; those who weren't directly affected by these negative things due to healthy economics, education, living location, etc., which are the runners who didn't collide with the block; those who were directly affected by the negative things but overcame them, which is the* *fallen victor; and people who purposely move towards these negative things even when they clearly have many other options, which are the runners running towards the stumbling block.*

1. In the analogy of the *Stumbling Block & The Fallen Victor* who do the marathon runners represent? _____

2. What does the stumbling block represent? _____
   _____

3. Name some examples of *fallen victors*? _____
   _____

4. Do you feel those who <u>finished</u> the marathon and **were unaffected** by the *stumbling block* should have gone back to help remove it? (remember you were on the same team) Why/Why not? _____
   _____
   _____

5. Do you feel those who <u>finished</u> the marathon and **were affected** by the *stumbling block* should have gone back to help remove it? (remember this was not a race/competition) Why/Why not? _____
   _____
   _____

6. Do you feel people from the hood who become financially successful should "give back" to those who are financially less fortunate than them? Why/Why not? _____
_____
_____

Define the following words.

Dependent: _____

Independent: _____

Interdependent: _____

7. Everyone needs some kind of help to be successful in life. Do you agree with this? Explain _____
_____
_____

8. Who do you feel should be responsible for funding youth programs like afterschool sports and tutoring and other social programs that serve the community? _____
_____

9. Who is responsible for teaching the community about how to make money legally and how money works? _____
_____

10. If you become financially successful, do you plan on "giving back?"
_____

11. What are some ways a person can "give back" other than monetary (money) hand outs? _____
_____
_____

12. In what ways do you feel older generations can help your generation?
_____
_____

13. In order to help others, it is good to identify your own gifts. What qualities, talents, and/or resources do you have that can be of benefit to your community? _____
_____
_____

Essay Prompt: If you were a millionaire with almost limitless resources, how would you help society?

Think About It: We are all *interdependent* on each other. No one gains success totally alone. Even the "Self-Made" got help from someone. Start giving back *today* in ways in which you are currently able.

"This some [stuff] I wrote about when I was broke,
  See the power of the mind is not a joke"

- Drake (Both)

Keep Your Next Move, Your Best Move
(Module Twelve)

The 2 Paths:

"If you don't know where you are going, any road can take you there."

There was a young man walking on a long journey. As he was walking, he arrived at a fork in the road. Confused about which path to take, he looked around and noticed a wise old man sitting quietly under a nearby tree. The young man walked to the wise old man and said, "Uh hi sir…I'm on a journey and I need help choosing which road to take. Will you help me decide?"

The wise old man asked, "Well, where are you going?" The young man said, "I don't know yet." The wise old man said, "Ok…Then either road will lead you to where you are going."

1. How do you think this story relates to you?

_____
_____
_____
_____

If you don't care much about your future, then all decisions you make today are ok. If, however, you *do* care about your future, then the decisions you make today will either move you closer to your goals or further away.

Picture yourself 5 years from now.

2. How old will you be? _____

3. What year will it be? _____

4. Where will you be living? (city/state) _____

5. What type of home? (dorms, studio, apartment, house) _____

6. What will you be doing? (will you have a job, be in school, or running your own business?) _____

7. How much money will you be earning per year? _____

If It Don't Make Dollars It Don't Make Sense

So how is one to legally secure financial stability? Well here's a secret:

According to Edward DeJesus, author of the book Makin' It, *the years of 14-26 are what he calls your* **Future Economic Opportunity** *(FEO) years. The author goes on to state that these are not your wealth building years...these are the years to position you for wealth building.* He goes further to explain that during your FEO years, you should focus on building the following:

- ✓ *Credentials (degrees, certificates)*
- ✓ *Skills (trades, training)*
- ✓ *Experience (job experience)*
- ✓ *Networks (meeting people with influence)*

I will add to this great list of essentials:
- ✓ *Knowledge (know how to do something)*
- ✓ *Character (good reputation)*

from Makin' It by Edward DeJesus

1. Without **any** of the six above resources in place, what resources do you have to help you build lasting wealth? _____
_____
_____

Remember, you can't cheat the grind. Many people want the hook up to getting opportunity and success. But even if a person gets a hook up, they still need to make sure that they are somehow qualified for the opportunity and can handle it properly.

2. Without **any** of the above in place, if you met a millionaire today and he/she wanted to recruit you for his/her company, what do you have to offer (other than being a hard worker and having a willingness to learn)?

_____
_____

3. Would it be wise to put someone without any of these in place in a position of authority in his/her millionaire company? Please explain.

_____
_____

4. Where will you be in two years if you start now focusing on positioning yourself to be wealthy in the future (credentials, skills, experience, network, knowledge and character)?

_____
_____
_____
_____

Think About It: What skills, experience and knowledge do you have or are currently working to develop? What credentials are you working towards? What influential people do you have in your network? What type of professional reputation are you creating?

Your degrees and credentials earned cannot be taken from you. Understand that obtaining a degree or credentials does not guarantee financial stability, but it has shown time and time again that it can be a valuable resource on the path to achieving financial stability.

The 4 Types of Money Makers

The world of economics is broken down into four types of people. They are employees, the self-employed, business owners and investors. None are better than the other. It all depends on what you want in life, what makes you happy and how you define success.

1. **Employees** *sell their time and skills. They often get paid an hourly wage to perform a task.*
2. The **self-employed** *owns a job. If they don't show up to their company no money can be made.*
3. **Business owners** *own a system that produces money even when they are not present*
4. **Investors** *sell money. They offer money to a business and receive interests or a percentage of the profits.*

Remember the list of essentials are credentials, skills, experience, networks, knowledge and character.

1. Of the list of essentials, which ones help you to be a successful employee? _____

2. Of the list of essentials, which ones help you to be successfully self-employed? _____

3. Of the list of essentials, which ones help you to be a successful business owner? _____

4. Of the list of essentials, which ones help you to be a successful investor? _____

_____

> # Education is the passport to the future, for tomorrow belongs to those who prepare for it today.
>
> -Malcolm X (El Hajj Malik El Shabazz)

1. Do you plan to attend college? _____

2. What are your career plans? _____

3. Describe the type of life you <u>plan</u> to live as an adult. _____
_____
_____
_____

4. How do you <u>plan</u> to achieve this life? _____
_____
_____

How Much Money Do I Really Need?

Let's calculate how much money you actually need to earn per month to live a basic lifestyle in today's society.

Monthly Expenses:

Rent/Mortgage	$_____	Internet	$_____
Electric Bill	$_____	Cable	$_____
Gas Bill	$_____	Recreation (*dates, parties, eating out, going to events, etc.*)	$_____
Car Note	$_____		
Car Insurance	$_____	Clothes	$_____
Groceries	$_____	Charity	$_____
Cell Phone Bill	$_____	Savings	$_____
Household Items (*soap, toothpaste, toilet paper, etc.*)	$_____	Gadgets (*computers, cell phone accessories*)	$_____
Hygiene (*haircut, cologne, etc.*)	$_____	(other)_____	$_____
		(other)_____	$_____

Monthly Total: $_____

x 12 = Yearly Total: $_____

Don't Blend In, Stand Out
(Module Thirteen)

Numbers Don't Lie

If you have dreams of being a professional athlete and have shared this dream with adults in your life, I'm sure you've heard how difficult it is to actually be selected to play at such a high, competitive caliber. Out of the hundreds and hundreds of thousands of young athletes who aspire to one day play sports on a professional level, below are the actual numbers of how many are chosen annually. Sharing these numbers with you are not meant to discourage you from pursuing your dream if this is what you want to do. Instead it is to help you understand how important it is for you to give your all and perform at your absolute best at all times.

NBA

The NBA draft is an annual event in which the **30** teams from the National Basketball Association (NBA) can draft players who are eligible and wish to join the league. These players are usually amateur U.S. college basketball players, but international players are also eligible to be drafted. The draft consists of **two** rounds, with each of the 30 teams getting one pick in each round. This makes a total of only **60** new players to be selected every year.

NFL

The National Football League (NFL) is a professional American football league composed of **32** teams divided equally between the National Football Conference (NFC) and the American Football Conference (AFC). This is highest level of professional football in the world. The National Football League draft, also called the player selection meeting, is an annual event in which the National Football League (NFL) teams select eligible college football players. It serves as the league's most common source of player recruitment.

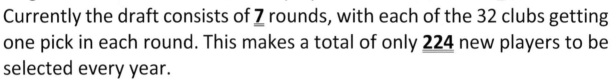

Currently the draft consists of **7** rounds, with each of the 32 clubs getting one pick in each round. This makes a total of only **224** new players to be selected every year.

NHL

The National Hockey League (NHL) operates a major professional ice hockey league of **30** franchised member clubs, of which seven are currently located in Canada and 23 in the United States. The NHL Entry Draft is an annual meeting in which every franchise of the National Hockey League (NHL) selects the rights to available amateur ice hockey players who meet draft eligibility requirements.

The NHL operates a **7**-round off-season draft. This makes a total of only approximately **210** new players to be selected every year.

MLB

Major League Baseball (MLB) is a professional baseball league consisting of teams that play in the American League and National League. It is composed of **30** teams, twenty-nine in the United States and one in Canada. Unlike most sports drafts, the First-Year Player Draft, MLB's entry draft, is held mid-season, in June. Another feature of this draft in is the draft lasts **40** rounds, plus compensatory picks, which makes the maximum total of new entries into the league well over **1000**. But all do not remain in the league. Many go to the minors and elsewhere.

So, here's a recap:

- The National Basketball Association drafts *60 new players each year*.

- The National Football League drafts *approximately 224 new players each year*.

- The National Hockey League drafts *approximately 210 new players each year*.

- Major League Baseball drafts *over 1000 new players each year*.

NOW for all of you who aspire to be a *professional* rapper...(professional meaning one who has made a **career** from rapping and is actually getting paid enough to live a comfortable life, being a rap artist), you may ask, "How do these sports statistics relate to Hip Hop?" Think about it. I mean seriously think about it. Have you ever seen *1000* new rappers enter the rap game in one year and make a solid career for themselves? How about *224* new rappers? Maybe *210* new rappers? Try *60* new rappers in one year?

I'm sure you realize by now that it's NEVER happened! As a matter of fact, if you start counting all the way back from the 1970's until our present day, I doubt if you can name a *total* of 200 financially successful rappers.

Even though the chances of a young athlete becoming a professional athlete are slim to none, statistically, you have a better chance of being drafted by the NBA, NFL, NHL or the MLB, than becoming a famous, and more importantly, financially successful rap star!

List as many **new** rappers as you can who released a **DEBUT** album on a major label last year.

_____
_____
_____

What is a record deal?

    A. A music contract that says a record label has to pay an artist for making music.

    B. A music contract that makes the record label rich and the artist broke.

    C. A music contract that documents the agreement made between a record label and an artist.

Music Business Mathematics

Gross: **income or profit without deduction of tax or other subtractions; total**

1. Let's say you are a rapper who sells 1,000,000 albums sold at $15.00 a piece. How much money is made? _____

2. According to your contract, the record label receives 25% of all ***gross sales***. How much money goes to the record label? _____

3. According to your contract, the distribution company receives 25% of all ***gross sales***. How much money goes to the distribution company? _____

4. According to your contract, your producer receives 40% of all ***gross sales***. How much money goes to the producer? _____

5. What percentage is left to pay you? (25% + 25% +40% = 90%) _____

6. How much money is this? _____

7. Oftentimes out of **your earnings**, *you* have to pay for studio time, video costs, wardrobe, party favors (alcohol, drugs, females, car rentals), hotel bills, photo shoots, clubbing, marketing & promotion. Let's say these total to $500,000 (this number varies depending on your taste). How much do you now have left? _____

8. Now you must pay 35% of your share (answer to #7) to the IRS. How much is this? _____

9. How much do you have now? _____
    (Remember, if you are in a group, you all have to split this. But for now, let's say you're a solo artist)

10. Out of the $ <u>15,000,000</u> made, you bring home $_____.

Now keep in mind that you receive this amount <u>only</u> if you go platinum (sell 1,000,000 albums). **Understand that due to piracy and free online access of music, the industry has changed, and consumers buy music less these days. Very few albums sell even a fraction of these numbers! It's sad that some artists find themselves <u>owing</u> the record labels money if their album doesn't sale enough.**

Many record labels are no longer in the *artist development* business. They are not looking for the next great artist that they can *make* a big star; they are looking for artists who currently have a fan base, hundreds of thousands of downloads and views of their online material and sold out live performances. Record labels seek to invest in artists who have already proven they are stars.

WORD OF ADVICE: Continue to pursue your dreams of being rich and famous, but make sure you also have a solid means to feed yourself and provide for your household.

Vocabulary List #11

Debut	Pivotal	Typical	Aspiration
	Society	Aspire	
Traditional	Entrepreneur	Appealing	Assembling
	Preparation	Maintain	Opportunity
		Motivation	

Legal Hustler

In 1993 Snoop Doggy Dogg released his debut album *Doggystyle*, which **debuted** at number one on the *Billboard* 200 chart, and sold almost one million copies in its first week alone. This was a record for a debuting artist release. We could talk in length about how **pivotal** this album was to the culture of Hip Hop. However, for this discussion, we will focus on a short but very important skit on the album. It is a skit that comes before the song *Gs and Hustlaz*. The setting takes place in an elementary classroom. The teacher, Mr. Buckwort, greets the young students, "*Good Morning boys and girls, I'm your Substitute teacher, Mr. Buckwort*." He goes on letting the young children know that the topic for the day is, "*What you wanna be when you grow up.*" Most of the children responded in the **typical** manner. One wanted to be a police officer, another a fire man, in which both responses received encouragement from the teacher. Then finally he calls on a young boy who is in the back of the class and described as wearing "French braids." Mr. Buckwort asks the young boy his name, in which he replies, "*My name is Snoop*." The teacher then asks young Snoop the question of the day: "*What do you want to be when you grow up?*" The young Snoop then answers with a golden response that represents the **aspirations** of thousands, if not millions, of young boys and girls growing up in the Hip Hop culture. His answer? "*I wanna be a hustla. You betta ask somebody.*"

For many people in our **society**, working a typical 9-5 job is a plan B or even plan C. Many aspire to be independent of the **traditional** clock in and clock out 8-hour, 5 day a week routine. We want to be bosses, owners...**entrepreneurs**. In other words, we want to be *hustlers*. To some people, working 40 hours a week for 30 years of our life and then retiring and receiving a percentage of our full salary does not seem **appealing**. Some dream of having an idea, putting together a strong team, turning that idea into a product or service and then selling that product or service to the world for hundreds of thousands or even millions of dollars! Many kids and adults daydream constantly about being their own boss. Unfortunately, oftentimes this is where it stops. Many never awake from their daydream to put their vision into practice. I've heard some people call successful businessmen and celebrities "lucky." However, when reading the background of many of these success stories we find that the "luck" that they experienced was that a different kind of luck. Have you ever heard the statement "*Luck is when opportunity meets preparation?*" Most successful individuals worked extremely hard to position themselves for their success and must continue to work hard to **maintain** it. Even for the few whom it may seem that an opportunity fell right in their laps, if they had not prepared themselves for the opportunity, that **opportunity** would be beyond their reach and would soon pass them by.

Being an entrepreneur requires major amounts of self-discipline. As an entrepreneur, you have no boss over your shoulder giving you deadlines. You must have self-**motivation** driving you to reach required deadlines of yourself. In the beginning stages, you will most likely be the hardest working individual in your company. Starting off you will probably be the inventor or service provider, you will also be the accountant, the tech guy, the head of marketing and promotions, saleswoman, the janitor and oftentimes, even the investor, which means you will be using your own money to finance the company! Sounds stressful...well it is. It's said that many entrepreneurs are willing to work 80 hours a week building their own business in order to avoid working 40 hours a week working for someone else and building their business.

Finally, what happens if you commit yourself to these duties and are rejected by people...meaning your fans don't support you like you hoped for? Or people don't show up to your grand opening like you expected? Or you don't get that deal that you were praying to make? Or people aren't willing to spend what you are charging? Now what? Do you quit? These are the battles successful hustlers have fought and overcome. Talk to any successful entrepreneur and they will tell you that failure is not losing. Quitting is losing. Failure is a part of the road to success. As a hustler, one must learn from past mistakes, perfect his hustle and keep it pushing! **(H.U.S.T.L.E. =** *How U Survive Through Life Everyday*)

1. According to the reading, what does being an entrepreneur require?
   _____

2. What does the statement "*Luck is when opportunity meets preparation*" mean?
   _____
   _____

3. The reading states "In the beginning stages, you will most likely be the hardest working individual in your company." What is meant by this?
   _____
   _____

4. "Failure is not losing. Quitting is losing." Do you agree with this? _____

5. How can failure be a part of "the road to success?" _____
   _____
   _____

6. After reading the many sacrifices involved with being a *boss*, do you prefer making a living as a business owner or an employee? Explain.
   _____
   _____

Are You an Entrepreneur?

This is an entrepreneur self-evaluation that will help you gain better insight to find out if you have the traits found in successful entrepreneurs. Read each question and circle the letter of the sentence that describes you the best.

1. **Are you a self-starter?**
   a. If someone helps me get started on a task, I will keep going to make sure I get the job done. (7 points)
   b. I usually start tasks on my own and like to do things my own way and come up with my own ideas about how to accomplish things. (10 points)
   c. I prefer to do no more than what is necessary. I really don't like putting myself in the forefront unless it is really necessary. (5 points)

2. **Are you a leader?**
   a. I usually like to let people lead themselves. (5 points)
   b. I can sometimes get people to do things but it's not easy to do this. (7 points)
   c. Most people go along with my ideas pretty easily. (10 points)

3. **How important is organization to you?**
   a. I like to make plans before I start something, and I stick to the plan until the job is done. (10 points)
   b. I go with the flow and like to take things as they come. I don't like to get boxed in with too many plans. (5 points)
   c. If things don't go according to my plan, I take this as a sign..."it wasn't meant to be". (7 points)

4. **How do you feel about people?**
   a. Most people irritate me. (5 points)
   b. I know enough people. I meet new people only when I feel it is totally necessary. (7 points)
   c. I really enjoy connecting with people and get along with others very well. (10 points)

5. **Are you a good worker?**
    a. I am willing to work hard until the goal is accomplished. I'll grind until the end. (10 points)
    b. I am willing to work hard if I know it will pay off right away. (7 points)
    c. I prefer not to work harder than I need to. I am very creative about coming up with ways so I don't have to work too hard. (5 points)

6. **How do you make decisions?**
    a. Before I make up my mind I like to check things out with my friends first. It is very important to know how they feel about my decisions. (7 points)
    b. I prefer to make my own decisions, I am willing to take responsibility for the consequences of my decisions. (10 points)
    c. I would rather have others make the decisions to make sure I don't make a mistake. (5 points)

7. **Are you trustworthy?**
    a. I try to avoid hurting people's feelings and say what I think they want to hear. (7points)
    b. I am usually very straightforward with what I have to say, even if other people may not agree with me. (10 points)
    c. I really don't care if people trust me. I do and say what I want. It doesn't matter much to me if it hurts others. (5 points)

8. **Do you see things to the end?**
    a. If I start a project I usually finish it. (7 points)
    b. If something goes wrong or is too difficult, I move on to something else. (5 points)
    c. If I set a goal and make up my mind to do something, I don't let anything stop me. (10 points)

9. **Do you choose to take responsibility?**
    a. I like to be in charge and make sure things get done. (10 points)
    b. I'll take charge if I have to but I prefer to let someone else be responsible (7 points)
    c. There's always a bossy person around. I prefer to let them do it. (5 points)

10. Is record keeping important to you?
   a. I understand the importance of record keeping, but it messes with my creativity. (7 points)
   b. Record keeping is very important to help me measure my success. (10 points)
   c. I keep records in my head and usually figure it out as I go. (5 points)

Look at your answers. Add the number of points in parenthesis after each of your answers. Use the totals below to describe how entrepreneurial you may be.

Find out where you fit on this scale:

(100-86) You have very strong entrepreneurial characteristics. Find out what you love to do and pursue it! Sounds like you have what it takes to become a successful entrepreneur.

(85-71) If you truly have a desire to be an entrepreneur and you scored in this range, find out what your weaknesses are and work to overcome them. Remember, confidence comes from learning to do things well.

(70-50) Sounds like you may want to think about working in a career where you are more secure and stable. The risks and commitment level required of an entrepreneur may be a bit challenging for you at this time in your life. If you want to pursue becoming more entrepreneurial, set some short-term goals and work towards accomplishing them.

Entrepreneurship: My Own Business

Executive Summary. In a few sentences explain your business.
_____
_____
_____

Business Name _____

What is the product or service you are offering? _____
_____
_____

Why is it needed/wanted? What problem is it solving? _____
_____
_____

What skills are required for this business? _____
_____
_____

How much does it cost to make? _____

How much are you selling your product or service for? _____
_____

Who is your competition? _____
_____
_____

What advantage do you have over your competition? _____
_____

Who is your target market? Describe your customers in detail.
(age, income, location, likes/dislikes, etc.)
_____
_____

What type of education is required? _____
_____
_____

What type of people do you need to know (network)? _____
_____
_____

What experience is required? _____
_____
_____

Who will run the business with you? _____
_____
_____

How much money will you make in the first year? _____
_____
_____

Know Better, Do Better

(Module Fourteen)

Did you know that

these entertainers went to college?

A look at a few rappers throughout Hip Hop history who attended college

Ludacris - Georgia State University

Chris Bridges attended Georgia State University where he graduated with a degree in music management. After graduating, he went on to co-found the company Disturbing Tha Peace Records with his manager Chaka Zulu.

David Banner - Southern University

Lavell Crump graduated from Southern University in Baton Rouge, Louisiana, where he majored in business. He was also the President of Student Government. After graduation from Southern University, he went on to pursue his Master's Degree in Education at the University of Maryland.

J. Cole - St. John's University

Jermaine Cole attended John's University in Queens, New York on an academic scholarship. There, he majored in communication and minored in business, graduating *magna cum laude.*

Lil' Wayne - University of Phoenix

D'Wayne Carter first attended the University of Houston where he studied psychology. He told the ladies of the television show "The View" that he began taking physical classes at University of Houston began to get "out of control," so he decided to switch to the online courses offered by University of Phoenix to complete his degree.

Talib Kweli - New York University
Talib Kweli Greene attended New York University where he graduated with a degree in experimental theater.

Plies - University of Central Florida & Miami University
Algernod Washington attended Miami University and played wide receiver on the football team during the year 1995-1997. He later transferred to the University of Central Florida, though he didn't complete his degree.

Kanye West - Chicago State University

Kanye West attended Chicago State University where he majored in English. West ended up leaving the school to pursue his career.

Diddy - Howard University

Sean Combs attended Howard University he majored in Business and became an intern at Uptown Records. He ended up dropping out of the university to pursue a career that eventually made him one of the wealthiest hip hop artists.

Common - Florida A&M University

Lonnie Lynn, Jr. attended Florida A&M University for two years under a scholarship where he studied business administration.

Find out which colleges the following artists attended.

"A lil G, never thought, that I could change the world with an attitude, a Raider jacket and a Jeri curl!"
(Dr. Frankenstein, 1998)

Ice Cube

_____

Fly Quote
"And you know I'm Anti, anti-social, anti-lame but ain't I cool, ….. ain't I?"
(Where You Been, 2013)

2Chainz _____

"I don't need no iron I'm already creased... [d]on't need no money I got mouthpiece!"
(Mouthpiece, 1999)

E-40 _____

Fly Quote
"Ain't nobody checking for your garbage lot of intuition, I ain't never finished college"
(Slight Work, 2011)

Wale _____

Career Research:

Answer these questions about a career of your choice.

Title of Occupation: _____

1. Description of the occupation including main duties and responsibilities.
   _____
   _____

2. What are the education and training requirements for this occupation?
   _____
   _____

3. List other required qualifications such as licensing, certifications, etc.
   _____
   _____

4. What is the average wage or salary for this occupation?
   _____

5. List the places and work environments where people in this occupation might work.
   _____
   _____

6. What are the opportunities for advancement?
   _____
   _____

7. List other occupations that are similar or related.
   _____
   _____

8. Is this occupation available in your area? List companies or other places of employment in your area in which this occupation is located.
   _____
   _____

9. What school subjects or courses would help you to prepare for this occupation?
   _____
   _____

10. Does this occupation deal mainly with people, data, things or ideas?
    _____
    _____

11. Do you think you have the aptitude (potential ability) for this occupation?
    _____
    _____

12. This occupation interests you because:
    _____
    _____

13. List three resources (books, magazines, internet, etc.) used for this research.
    _____
    _____

14. List the name of a person(s) you know (or know of) who is in this occupation.
    _____
    _____

My Chosen Profession

You can do this assignment in your workbook or on a separate sheet of paper.

Paragraph 1
State and describe the profession you want to pursue. What skills are needed for this profession? What characteristics are necessary?

_____
_____
_____
_____
_____

Paragraph 2
Describe a day in the life of yourself in this profession. What sacrifices need to be made? What habits must you have?

_____
_____
_____
_____
_____

Paragraph 3
Why did you choose this profession? How does who you are as a person relate to this profession? Why will you be good at this profession?

_____
_____
_____
_____
_____

Wealth Mindset
(Module Fifteen)

"Financial freedom my only hope, [forget] living rich and dying broke"

-Jay Z

Vocabulary List #12

wealth	generation	legacy	perceive	interpret
impact	navigate	immediate	quality	benefit
	consciousness	poverty		

Generational Wealth

Have you ever heard of "generational wealth?" Generational wealth is wealth made in one or more generations and kept in the family over time, like the Rockefellers. Generational Wealth is about *honoring your family name*. Building generational wealth often occurs over many lifetimes. If asked "What is your great great grandfather's name?" Many of us would say, "I do not know." The reason is because we may not be connected to a family legacy.

As we navigate through life, many tend to only think about our immediate situation. Although this is important, it is also important to think ahead—*far into the future.* In building generational wealth and creating a strong family legacy, we must ask ourselves, "How will my grandchildren and great-grandchildren benefit from what I am doing today?" "What impact will my decisions have on their quality of life?" "What will they be told about me?"

Building generational wealth is about more than just money. It is about building wealth in values, beliefs, traditions, network, knowledge and reputation. Your thoughts become your beliefs and your actions. It is important to take responsibility for what happens to you in your life. Blaming others may sometimes temporarily make you feel better about unwanted conditions in your life, but it also robs you of your personal power. How we experience the world is directly related to our own mind. It's usually not what happens in the world, but how we perceive, interpret and respond to what happens that matters most. Through the way we think, the attitude we have and the actions we take, we have the ability to change our lives. That is the personal power you have.

Building generational wealth is about building on the financial success of past generations. The Rockefellers, Kennedys, Hiltons, and Marriotts are examples of families who have passed down wealth for generations. Everyone needs an income. For some it's a job. For others, it's a career and for some it's being an entrepreneur and building a business. Some people think they have a business when in reality, they have simply created a job for themselves. Either way, money is important. However, when building generational wealth, we must not only think about *making* money, we must also think about what to do with it once we get it. Do you make money and then spend it? Do you invest it in assets? Assets are property owned by a person or company that has value and often creates generates income.

Poverty consciousness is also often passed down from generation to generation. Poverty consciousness is a set of attitudes, beliefs, feelings and values that focuses on material lack or fear of material lack. Many of us have inherited our perspectives about money and wealth from our families. That can be a strength or a weakness depending on what money lessons we have been taught. We all grew up watching parents say and do certain things certain ways. Maybe you thought what they were doing was great and want to do the same, or maybe you have decided that change is needed. If what you have been taught leads to poverty, then it is your own responsibility to make sure you do not travel through life with the same bad habits your family practiced. No need to blame your family for bad habits. Instead make it a point to shift your mindset, focus on your situation, focus on your goals, and do what is best for you and your family. You must decide to be successful and create a plan if you want to succeed in making that change. Generational wealth can only begin when we erase the poverty consciousness that can create *generational poverty* and replace it with the financial education. Even if all you want to do is carry forward an already established legacy of wealth building, you need a plan to protect and grow your generation's efforts.

Investing in assets is an important means to creating ways to pass on wealth to future generations. Spending too much money on things that do not generate income can destroy your opportunities for passing on wealth to future generations. Building generational wealth doesn't happen overnight. It requires a long-term commitment of saving and investing and establishing expectations in the family to help out the next generation.

None of us want spoiled rich brats in the family, but we do want to give our kids a good start in life, perhaps a better one than we had. Developing a plan to get your own wealth is a start, but if you think past the next two generations to the third one, you will be well on the way to building a wealthier future for your family. Your plan doesn't necessarily have to be all about getting money, it can be about giving your children and grandchildren more opportunities, better examples, increased education, knowledge and a strong network. These things can result in your kids getting a great start and helps them to make more, save more, invest more and build their generation's wealth.

Your plan shouldn't be about how to get rich fast. Most people don't succeed at getting rich quick. But many of us can succeed with a get rich slow approach. We can all step by step increase our own wealth with the intentions of passing it to the next generation.

1. What is "generational wealth?" _____
   _____
   _____

2. What are some valuable things that can be passed down from generation to generation?
   - _____
   - _____
   - _____
   - _____
   - _____

3. Is generational wealth important? Why? _____
   _____
   _____

4. How does one's life who receives generational wealth differ from those who don't receive it? _____
   _____
   _____

5. How is generational wealth created? _____
   _____
   _____

6. What are some examples of "assets?" _____

_____

_____

7. What is "poverty consciousness?" _____

_____

_____

8. Do you plan to pass generational wealth to your children? Why/Why Not?

_____

_____

9. Money can be *spent* or *invested*. What does this statement mean?

_____

_____

_____

10. What are some ways money can be spent? _____

_____

_____

11. What are some ways money can be invested? _____
_____
_____

Personal Mission Statement

Create a mission statement for yourself. Write a vision that is rooted in your values and speaks of your plans for future success. Whatever is high on your list of values should somehow be stated in your mission statement. For example, if you value helping others or being financially successful, this should be included in your mission statement.

Ex: *It is my mission to live a life of service, integrity, prosperity and happiness. I am committed to both the physical, mental and spiritual well-being of myself and the physical, mental and spiritual well-being of others.*

_____
_____
_____
_____
_____

List Some Routes One Can Take to Be Financially Successful:

1. Entertainment/Sports Industry

2. _____

3. _____

4. _____

Definiteness of Purpose

Remember, a goal is a promise to yourself

What is your "carrot?" What motivates you to move forward?

1. What are three definite steps necessary to take in order to achieve your goal? _____
   _____
   _____
   _____

2. What obstacles must you overcome to achieve your goal?
   _____
   _____
   _____

3. Who will help you achieve your goal? _____
   _____
   _____

4. Why did you choose them to help you achieve your goal? What qualities do they possess? _____
   _____
   _____
   _____

5. In what ways will they help you? _____
   _____
   _____
   _____

6. What must you sacrifice to achieve your goal? _____
   _____
   _____
   _____

7. Why do you want to achieve your goal? _____
   _____
   _____
   _____

8. When do you plan to have your goal accomplished?
   _____
   _____
   _____

Remember, if you do not have a vision for your life, someone else will have you living theirs.

Forward Movement
(Module Sixteen)

Question:

There were 3 Cats Sitting on A Wall. 2 decide to jump off. How many are left sitting on the wall?

Answer:

Still 3! Just because they _decided_ to jump off the wall doesn't mean they actually _did_ it.

Point:

There are many people who _decide_ to do many things in life, but never _act_ on it and remain in the same place.

Decisions & Actions

Write a decision and action you can make right now to work towards overcoming each of the obstacles you listed. (*ex. Decision: I am deciding to go to college/ Action: I will go to my high school classes everyday*) **Note: The decision is the goal, the action is the method of achieving the decision/goal**

Decision: _____
_____

Action: _____
_____

Decision: _____
_____

Action: _____
_____

Decision: _____
_____

Action: _____
_____

Decision: _____
_____

Action: _____
_____

Decision: _____
_____

Action: _____
_____

Decision: _____
_____

Action: _____
_____

Decision: _____
_____

Action: _____
_____

Decision: _____
_____

Action: _____
_____

The Gate of Obstacles

What keeps you from accomplishing your financial goals? (i.e. laziness, lack of education, lack of motivation, criminal record, etc.)

Write up to 8 obstacles that are in the way of your success in the boxes above.

1. Have you missed out on anything because of these obstacles? If so, what?
_____
_____
_____
_____

2. How do these obstacles affect the lives and/or feelings of your loved ones?
_____
_____
_____
_____

3. What kind of life can you have if you learn and commit to overcoming these obstacles?_____
_____
_____
_____

4. How could your refusal to overcome these obstacles affect your future?
_____
_____
_____
_____

5. How will keeping these obstacles in your life benefit your life or the lives of the people you love?

_____
_____
_____
_____

6. How will you feel knowing you have overcome these obstacles?

_____
_____
_____
_____

7. How will overcoming these obstacles help you have a successful life?

_____
_____
_____
_____

8. How will you overcoming these obstacles affect your loved ones feelings?

_____
_____
_____
_____

My Goal

One a separate sheet of paper, in two paragraphs, write about your current purpose/goal. In your writing, answer the following questions: *What purpose are you living? (What goal are you seeking to accomplish?) What motivates you to live this purpose? Where did you get this purpose from? Who or what taught you that you should live this purpose? How does this purpose make you feel about yourself? Who does this purpose benefit? In what ways is this purpose beneficial?*

Here's how to do it...

Sentence Order	Example
Begin with a statement that gets the reader's attention	*I've noticed that many people are still searching for their goal.*
Support your first sentence	*Finding your passion is sometimes very difficult to do.*
State your purpose/goal	*Luckily, I have decided that my goal is to graduate high school and earn a college degree.*
State what motivates you to live this purpose	*I know that in order to be successful in life, I'm going to need an education.*
Follow up your previous sentence	*I'm not sure if I want to go to a four year university, but I know I at least want to graduate from a community college.*
State where you got this purpose/goal from. Who or what	*My mom has always told me that education is important.*

taught you that you should pursue this goal?	
State how does this goal/purpose make you feel about yourself.	*Knowing that I am planning to go to college, makes me feel good about myself.*
Support your previous sentence	*This goal gives me something to look forward to.*
State who this purpose/goal benefits	*Going to college will benefit me and my family.*
Support your previous sentence, by stating how this purpose/goal is beneficial	*It will benefit me because I will use my education to get a good job and help take care of my family.*

Live Above the Hype:
Choose to Be Your Best Self Regardless of Popular Opinion

Glossary

Glossary

Accomplish - achieve or complete successfully

Acknowledge - to recognize; to disclose knowledge of; to take notice of

Agile - able to move quickly and easily

Aggressive - ready or likely to attack or confront

Allegory - a story in which the characters and events are symbols that stand for ideas about human life

Allure - to entice by charm or attraction

Alternative - different from the usual or conventional

Anthem - a song that is very important to a particular group of people

Appealing - attractive or interesting

Appropriate - right or suited for some purpose or situation

Aspect - a part of something

Aspire - direct one's hopes or ambitions toward achieving something

Assembling - (of people) gather together in one place for a common purpose

Aspiration - a hope or ambition of achieving something

Benefit - an advantage or profit gained from something

Bitterness - angry and unhappy, usually due to perceived unfair treatment

Glossary

C

Calamity - an event that causes great harm and suffering

Caliber - level of excellence, skill, etc.

Chauvinism - an attitude that the members of your own sex are better than or superior to those of the opposite sex

Community - a group of people who live in the same area, or who have the same interests, religion, race, etc.

Compromise - a way of reaching agreement in which each person or group gives up something that was wanted in order to end an argument or dispute

Confrontational - tending to deal with situations in an aggressive way; hostile or argumentative

Condemn - to say in a strong and definite way that someone or something is bad or wrong

Conquer - overcome and take control of (a place or people) by use of force

Conscious - aware of and responding to one's surroundings; awake

Consciousness - the awareness or perception of something by a person

Contempt - a feeling that someone or something is not worthy of any respect or approval

Glossary

Controversial - relating to or causing much discussion, disagreement, or argument

Criticize - to express disapproval of (someone or something) : to talk about the problems or faults of (someone or something)

D

Debut - a person's first appearance or performance in a particular capacity or role.

Deceptive - intended to make someone believe something that is not true

Deity - one exalted or revered as supremely good or powerful; a god or goddess

Denounce - to publicly state that someone or something is bad or wrong: to criticize (someone or something) harshly and publicly

Dependent - requiring someone or something for financial, emotional, or other support.

Deteriorate - to become worse as time passes

Detrimental - causing damage or injury; harmful

Devotion - a feeling of strong love or loyalty: the quality of being devoted

Dialogue - a conversation between two or more people

Glossary

Dictate - to say or state (something) with authority or power; to make (something) necessary

Discrimination - the practice of unfairly treating a person or group of people differently from other people or groups of people

Disperse - to cause to become spread widely

Distribution - the act of giving or delivering something to people, a store or business

Divisive - causing a lot of disagreement between people and causing them to separate into different groups

Doctrine - a set of ideas or beliefs that are taught or believed to be true

Dominate - to have control of or power over (someone or something)

Dysfunction - the condition of having poor and unhealthy behaviors, attitudes   or interactions within a group of people;

E

Effective - producing a result that is wanted : having an intended effect

Emancipation - the act of freeing (someone) from someone else's control or power

Enchanted - fill (someone) with great delight; charm; put someone under a spell

Glossary

Entrepreneur - a person who organizes and operates a business or businesses, taking on greater than normal financial risks in order to do so

Euphoria - a feeling of great happiness and excitement

Exclude - to leave out (something or someone): to not include (something or someone)

External - of or situated on the outside

F

Frequency - the number of times that something happens during a particular period

Fulfill - to satisfy; to succeed in achieving (something

G

Generation - all of the people born and living at about the same time

Genocide - the deliberate killing of people who belong to a particular racial, political, or cultural group

Glossary

H

Hasten - to move or act quickly; to cause something to act or move quickly

Heroic - having the characteristics of a hero or heroine; very brave

Hinder - create difficulties for (someone or something), resulting in delay of progress

Honor - to show admiration for (someone or something) in a public way; to regard or treat (someone) with respect and admiration; to do what is required by (something, such as a promise or a contract)

I

Ideology - the set of ideas and beliefs of a group or political party; manner or the content of thinking characteristic of an individual, group, or culture

Illusory - based on something that is not true or real

Imagination - the ability of the mind to be creative or resourceful

Immediate - occurring or done at once; instant

Impact – to have a strong effect on someone or something

Glossary

Impulsive - doing things or tending to do things suddenly and without careful thought: acting or tending to act on impulse

Independent - not depending on another for livelihood or subsistence.

Intensify - to become stronger or more extreme: to become more intense

Interdependent - (of two or more people or things) dependent on each other

Internal - of or situated on the inside

Interpret - explain the meaning of (information, words, or actions)

Intrigue - to make (someone) want to know more about something: to cause (someone) to become interested

Ironic - strange or funny because something (such as a situation) is different from what is naturally expected

J

Judgment - an opinion or decision that is based on careful thought; the act or process of forming an opinion or making a decision after careful thought

Glossary

Lease - a legal agreement that lets someone use a possession (such as a car or house), for a period of time in return for payment

Legacy - anything handed down from the past, as from an ancestor to present and future generations

Libation - a liquid that is poured out to honor a god or an ancestor (one who has passed away)

Maintain - cause or enable (a condition or state of affairs) to continue

Manipulate - to control or play upon by artful or unfair means, especially to one's own advantage

Mantra - a word or phrase that is repeated often or that expresses someone's basic beliefs

Marathon - a long-distance race; an endurance contest

Martyr - person who is killed or who suffers greatly for a religion, cause, principle, etc.

Glossary

Materialism - a way of thinking that gives too much importance to material possessions rather than to spiritual or intellectual things

Meditation – the act of thinking deeply or focusing one's mind for a period of time, in silence or with the aid of chanting, for religious, spiritual or health purposes or as a method of relaxation

Moral - concerning or relating to what is right and wrong in human behavior

Motivation - the reason or reasons one has for acting or behaving in a particular way

Mundane - lacking interest or excitement; dull

N

Navigate - to direct or manage something on its course

Negotiate - to discuss something formally in order to make an agreement

Glossary

O

Observer - a person who sees and notices someone or something

Obstacle - something that makes it difficult to do something; an object that you have to go around or over; something that blocks your path

Opportunist - someone who tries to get an advantage or something valuable from a situation without thinking about what is fair or right

Opportunity - a set of circumstances that makes it possible to do something; a chance for employment or promotion

P

Parable - a short story that teaches a moral or spiritual lesson

Perceive - interpret or look on (someone or something) in a particular way

Perspective - one's point of view

Pivotal - of crucial importance in relation to the development or success of something else

Potential - The inherent ability or capacity for growth, development, or coming into being

Poverty - the state of being extremely poor

Glossary

Prelude - an action or event serving as an introduction to something more important

Preparation - the action or process of making ready or being made ready for use or consideration

Privatize - to remove (something) from government control and place it in private control or ownership

Procrastinate - to be slow or late about doing something that should be done; to delay doing something until a later time because you do not want to do it, because you are lazy, etc.

Productive - producing or able to produce something especially in large amounts; causing or resulting in something

Progression - the process of developing over a period of time; a continuous and connected series of actions, events, etc.

Prosperity - the state of being successful usually by making a lot of money

Provoke - deliberately make (someone) annoyed or angry

Quality – a distinctive attribute or characteristic possessed by someone or something; the standard of something as measured against other things of a similar kind

Glossary

R

Recreation - something people do to relax or have fun; activities done for enjoyment

Rehabilitate - to teach (a criminal in prison) to live a normal and productive life; to bring (someone or something) back to a good condition

Refrain - to stop yourself from doing something that you want to do

Reinforce - to encourage or give support to (an idea, behavior, feeling, etc.)

Relegate - to put (someone or something) in a lower or less important position, rank, etc.; to give (something, such as a job or responsibility) *to* another person or group

Restitution - payment that is made to someone for damage, trouble, etc.

Ridicule - the act of making fun of someone or something in a cruel or harsh way: mean or unkind comments or behavior

Rites of Passage - A ritual or ceremony signifying an event in a person's life indicative of a transition from one stage to another, as from adolescence to adulthood

Glossary

Ritual - a formal ceremony or series of acts that is always performed in the same way; an act or series of acts done in a particular situation and in the same way each time

Revolve - to turn around a center point or line

S

Significant - sufficiently great or important to be worthy of attention; noteworthy

Society - an organized group of persons associated together for religious, benevolent, cultural, scientific, political, patriotic, or other purposes; a body of individuals living as members of a community

Sole - being the only one; only

Standard - an idea or thing used as a measure, norm, or model in comparative evaluations.

Subjected - Being in a position or in circumstances that place one under the power or authority of another or others

Suburban - a residential district located on the outskirts of a city

Sway - to influence or move something or someone to one side or in a particular direction

Glossary

T

Traditional - habitually done, used, or found; existing in or as part of a tradition; long-established

Transform - make a thorough or dramatic change in the form, appearance, or character of

Transformation - to change in form, appearance, or structure, condition, nature, or character

Typical - showing all the characteristics that you would usually expect from a particular group

U

Untamed - not domesticated or controlled

Urban - Of, relating to the city life

Glossary

Values - Important beliefs shared by the members of a culture about what is good or bad and what is desirable or undesirable. Values have major influence on a person's behavior and attitude and serve as broad guidelines in all situations

Vivid - producing powerful feelings or strong, clear images in the mind.

Wealth - an abundance of valuable possessions or money; the value of all the property, possessions, and money that someone or something has

Acknowledgements

This book, along with the Facilitator's Manual, was written with a heart set on empowering our youth to live fuller and dream bigger. Outside of first and foremost, GOD, I would like to take this time to thank a few people who were very instrumental in making this book a reality: Queen Angie V... Thank you for your patience, understanding and constant encouragement throughout this entire process; Chris Finney, my brotha...who has supported everything I have put my hand to. Salute! Forward Movement! Kimmie....my comrade...Thank you so much for all that you have done and continue to do to support this work and helping it expand across the nation. Dr. Michael Eric Dyson, the God-Father of Hip Hop Academia. It was through you where I first saw that Hip Hop culture had an authentic place in intellectual, academic thought. Thank you for taking the time to reach out and for being so generous with sharing the influence of your social celebrity, not only with me, but also with the many other young brothas and sistas you support and endorse. Salute! Professor Najeeba-Syeed Miller, the time, the insight and the encouragement you have blessed me with is certainly appreciated. Thank you. Diana White, thank you for your love and being my first teacher and instilling in me to "Do it right, or don't do it all!" Adam Steel...What an awesome book trailer. Brotha I appreciate you stepping in the trenches with me to make sure this book was represented to the world at the highest quality on camera. John & Carolyn Griffin, thank you for igniting the flame. Those cassette tapes of the Front Page and that copy of the Willie Lynch Letter really did a number on me. My twin Nico White...you always got my back bro. Much love. We almost there! Tony Massengale (Rest In Peace), thank you for teaching me the importance of collaboration and being so willing to share your knowledge and network with me and others in this struggle for Peace. Willa Robinson...your insight and prayers have been a blessing. Brian Biery, thanks for being there to plug me in with the right people I need for the next step. Raheem Noel, Bro...good looking out on giving me my first book on Knowledge of Self, The Browder Files, and encouraging me to read it, even when I let it get dusty on my coffee table. Salute! Fidel Rodriguez...I appreciate you sticking to your vision and being such a trailblazer in this quest and struggle to "de-colonize minds." Omowale Ujamaa Shule for embedding in me at a very young age the wise words, "One who learns, must teach." Salvatrice Cummo thank you for being there when I need quick witted insight. Alvin and Sabrina Edington...Yo! Thanks for your input in helping entitling this book. Jen Hanson...You're an all-star!! Thank you so much the work and brain power you put in to make sure this book properly present to the world! Dumas Martin...the wisdom you share with me is very much appreciated. Mike Harris...this is just the beginning brotha. RaeShelle Green...Thanks for your insight and laughs throughout this process. Much needed! Kevin & Danielle Jackson...thanks for always being there supporting this cause. Fate Hagood III...I appreciate your awesome trailblazing leadership. Brotha Boko & Auntie Akilah...You have been a mentor to me throughout the years. I appreciate you sharing with me the importance of Life. Light. Love and Peace. Salute! Ayele & Azuri...I love you and thank God for you.

And to the many Brothas and Sistas who have supported me and to those who have made a commitment to stand for the betterment of others. Let's take tha corners back!!! (*For those who know*). Peace

Made in the USA
Monee, IL
09 January 2025

74268235R00109